Lazy Day Coloring Book

Lazy Day Coloring Book

David L Smith
&
William L. Sharrar

To order additional copies of this book, contact:
Xlibris Corporation
1-888-795-4274
www.Xlibris.com
Orders@Xlibris.com
83398

Dedication

We dedicate this book to young and old everywhere, in hope that one would find pleasure and enjoyment as to what their mind will create. May your colors of your creation shine for others to see. We hope that you enjoy your new coloring book as much as we did making it.

God bless,
Dave & Bill

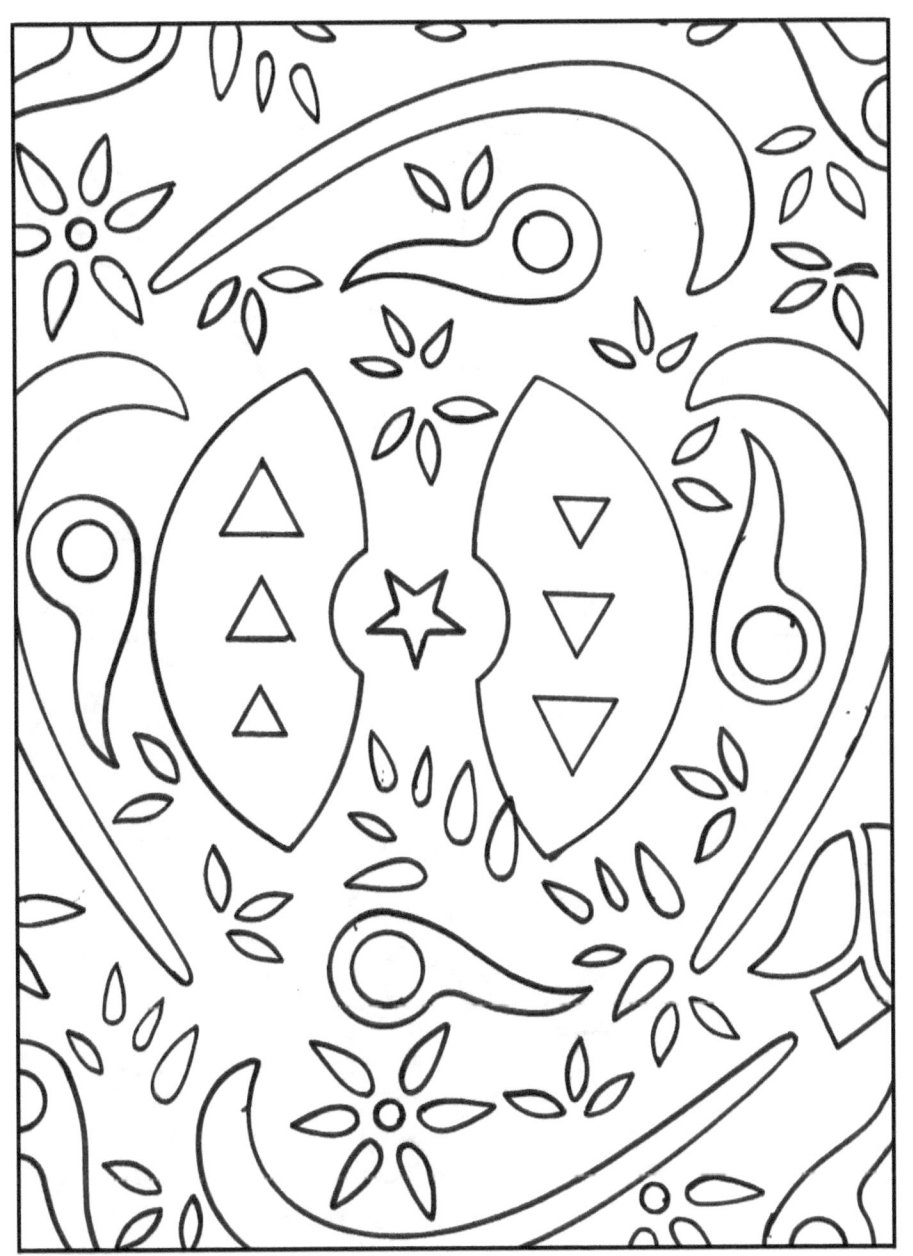

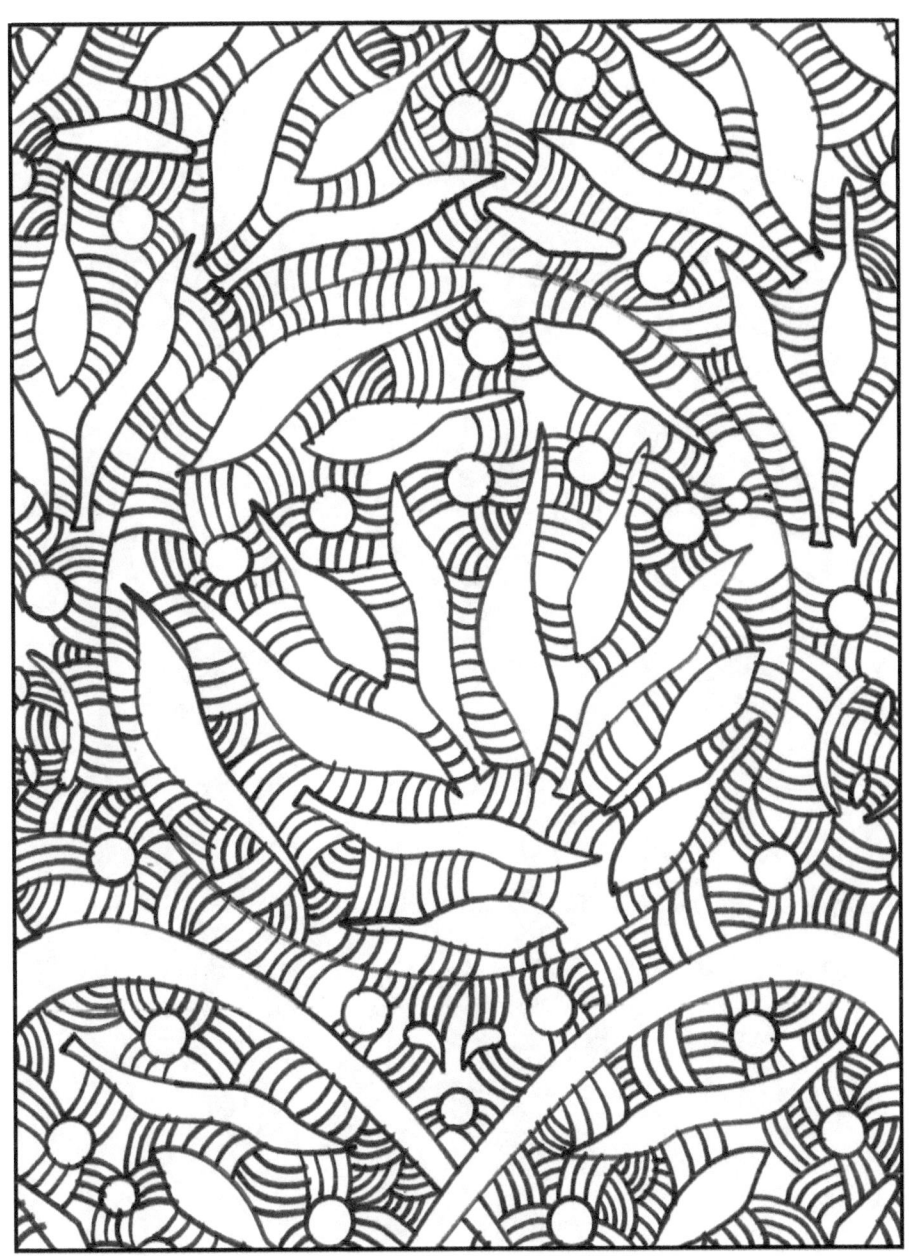

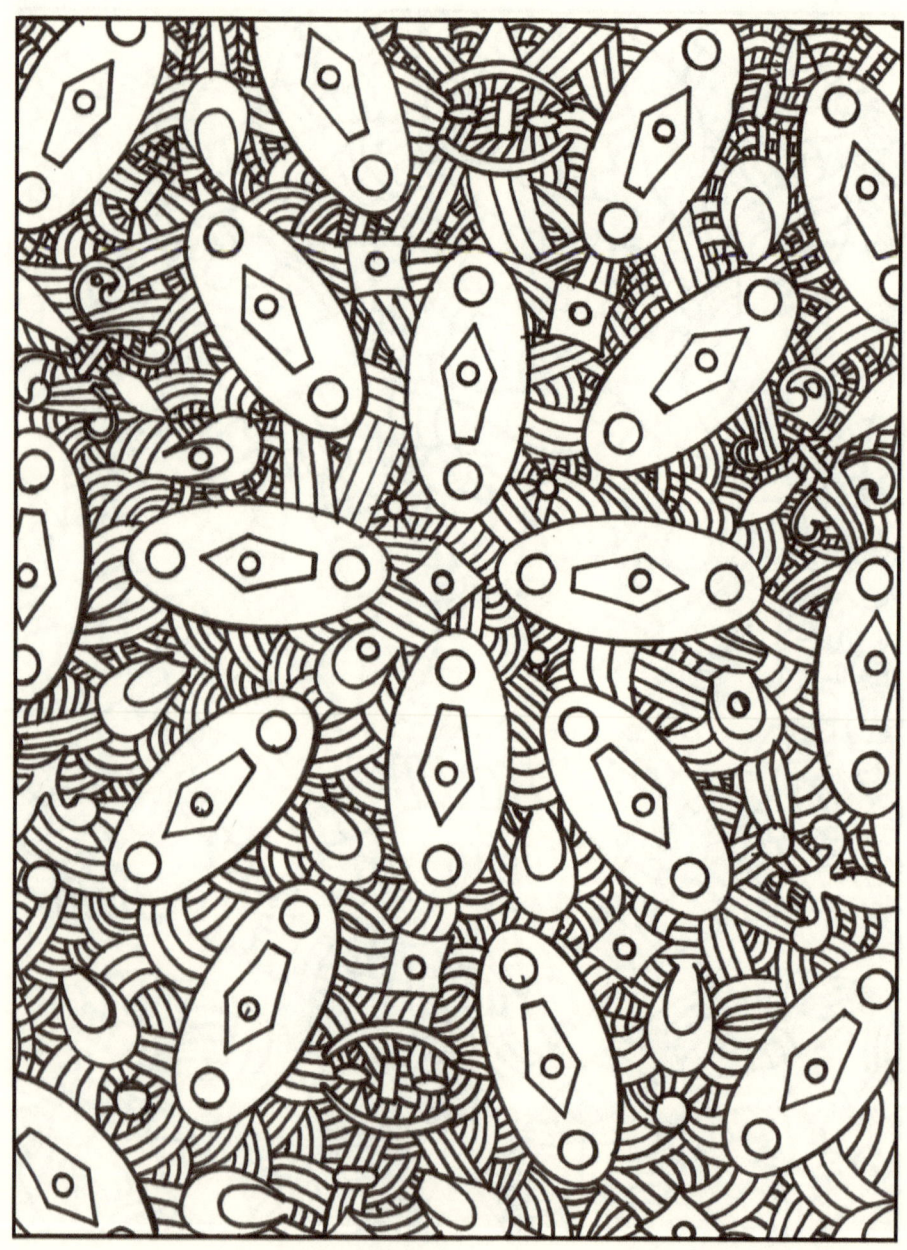

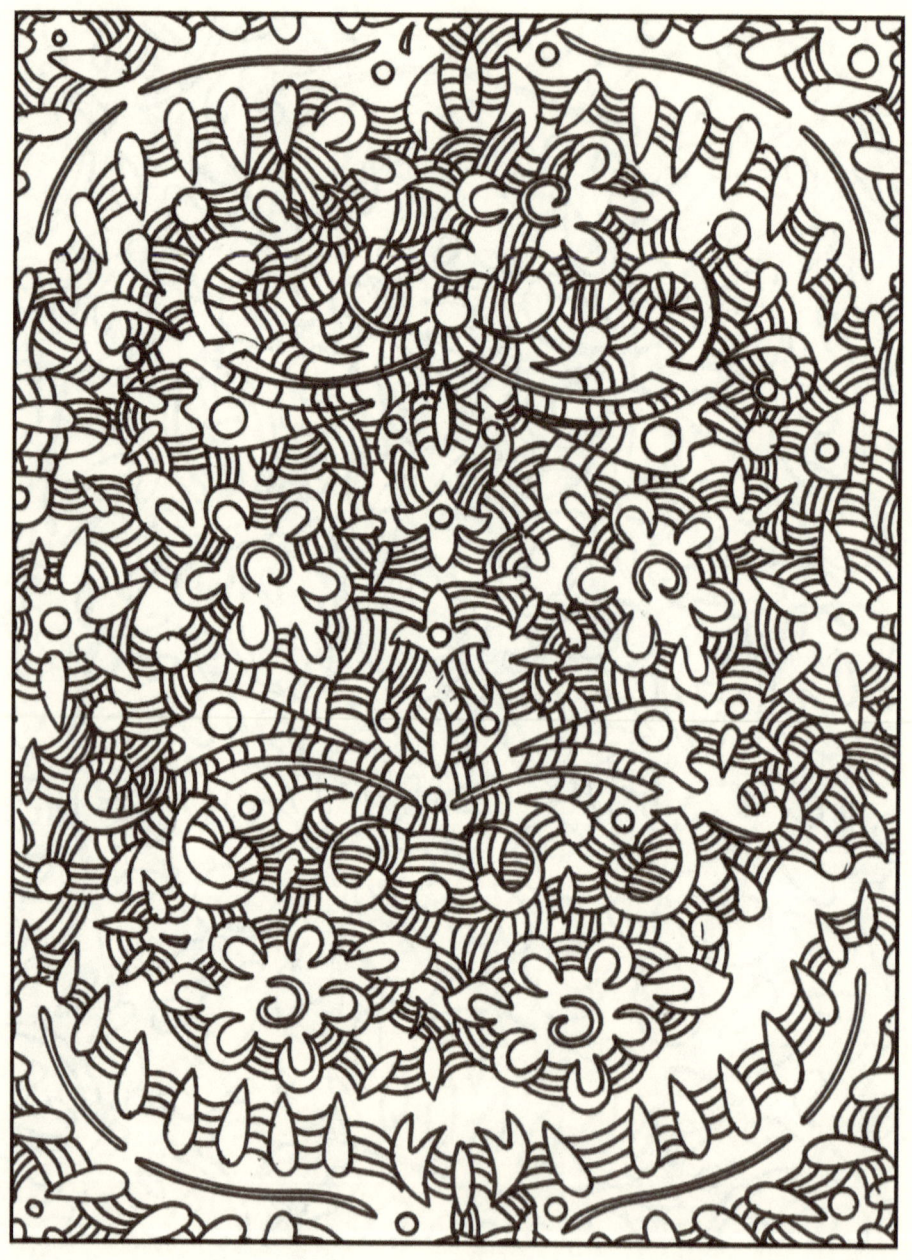

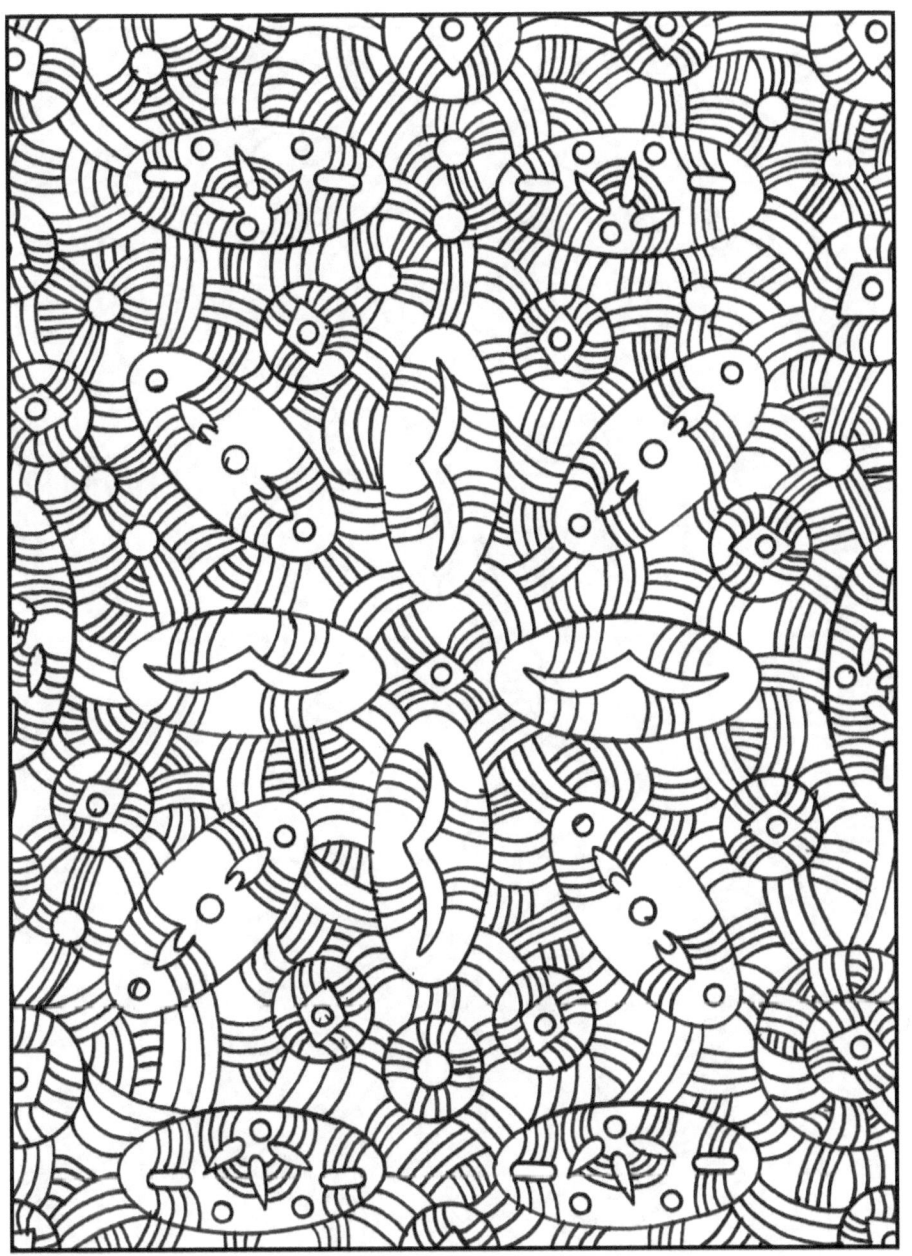

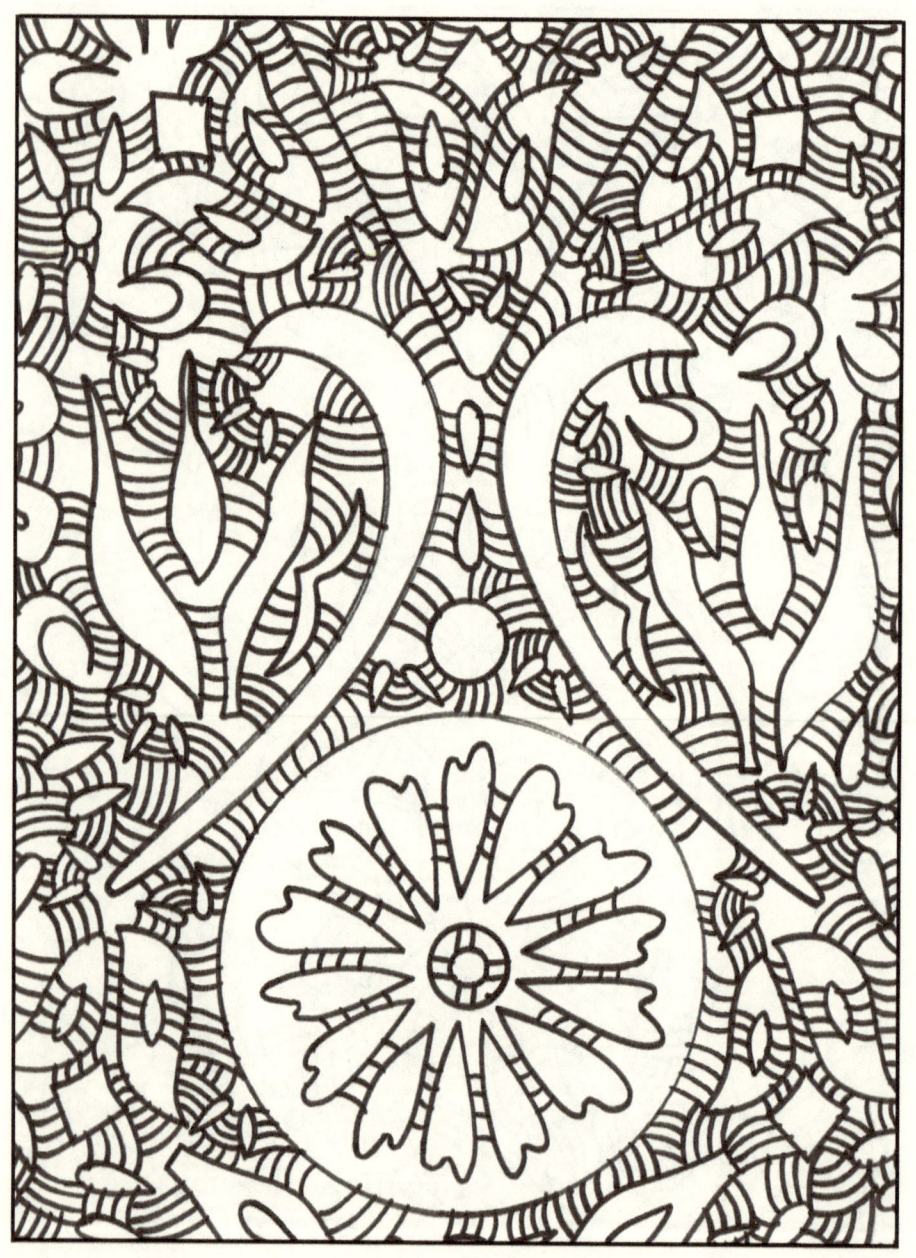

14

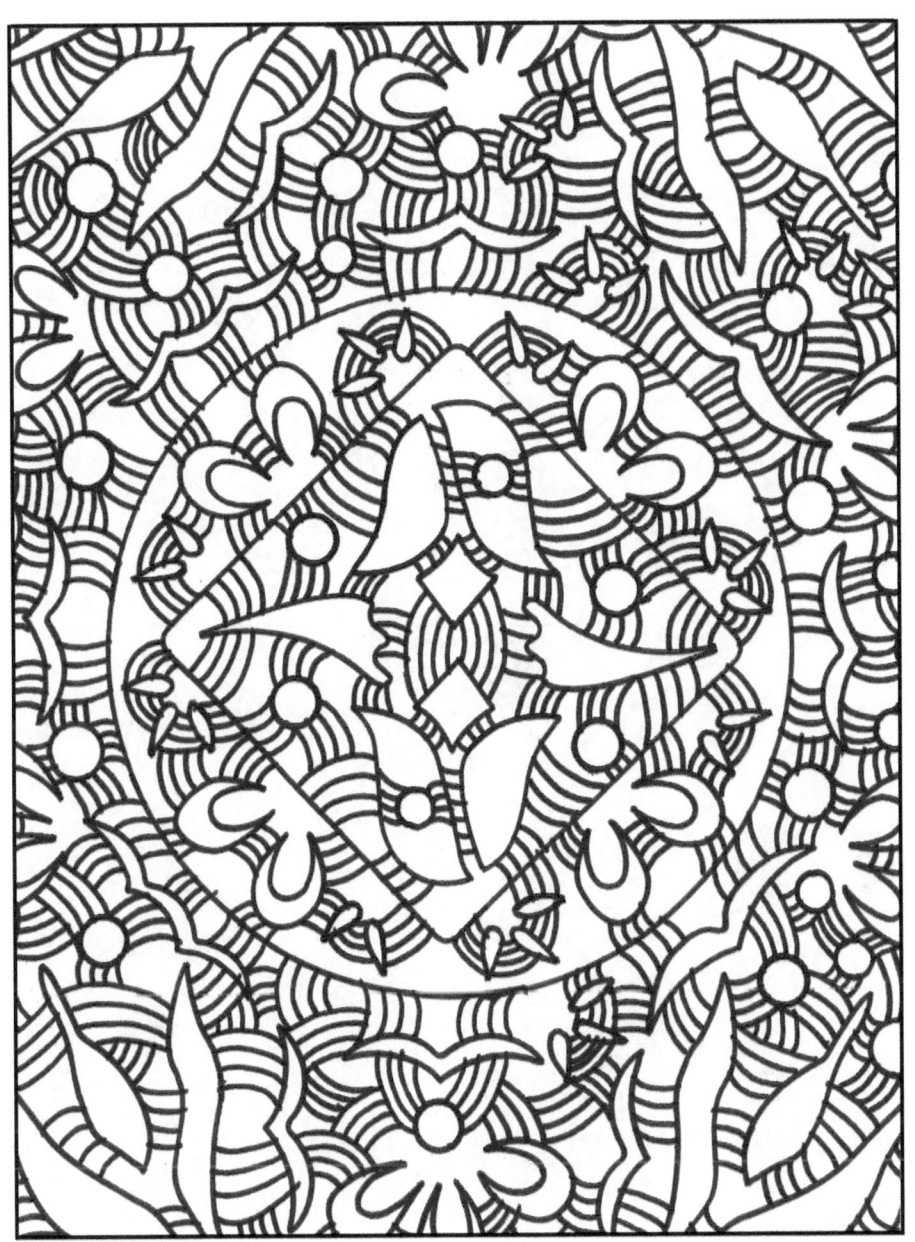

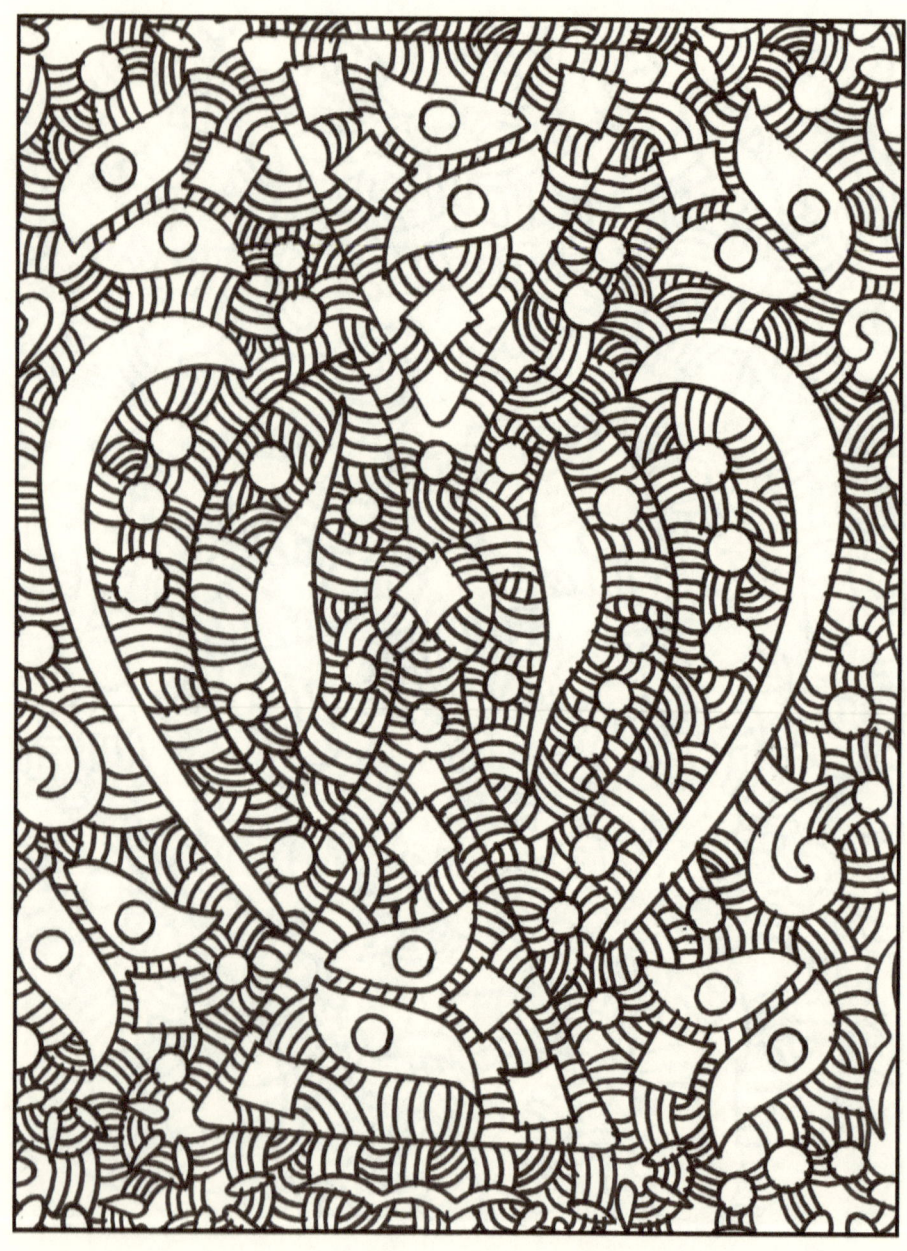

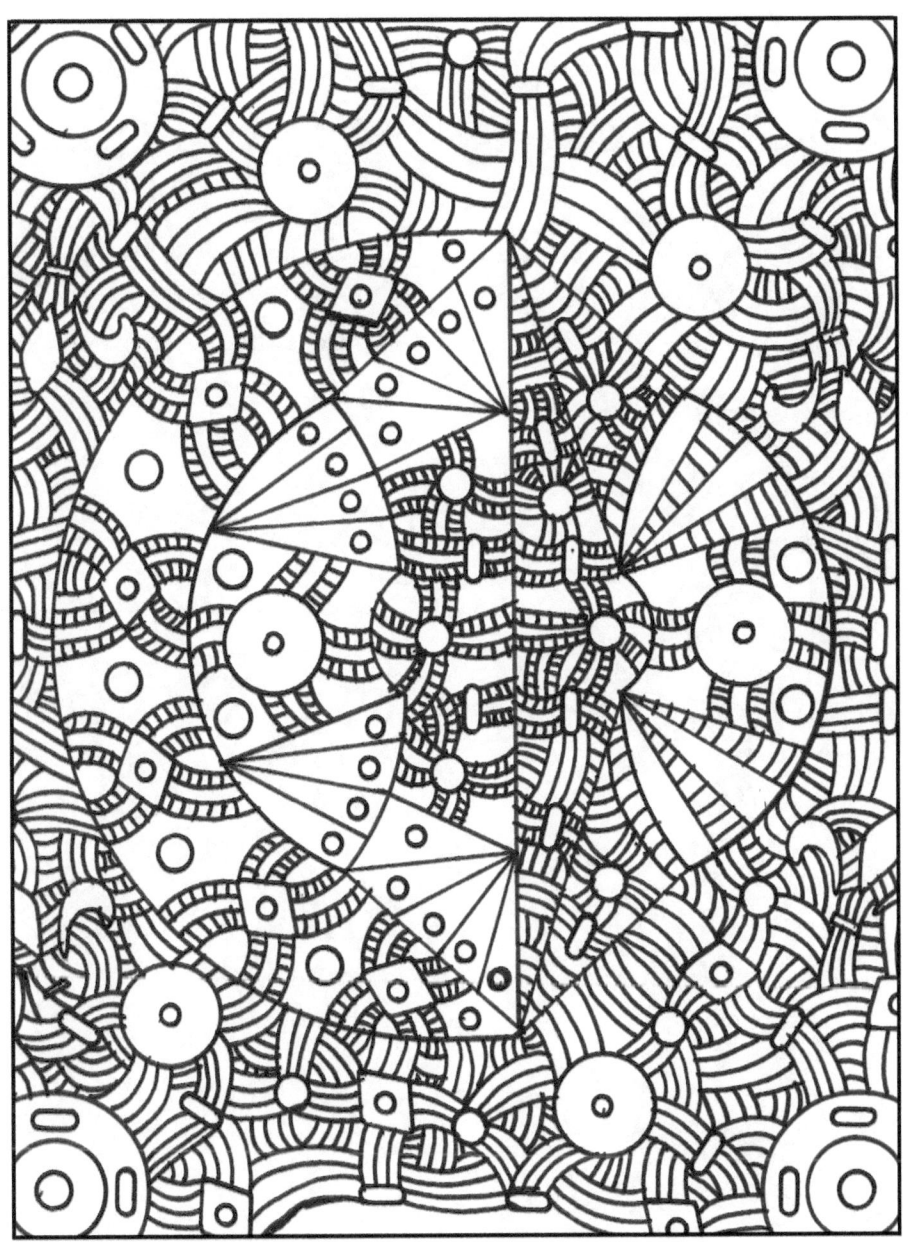

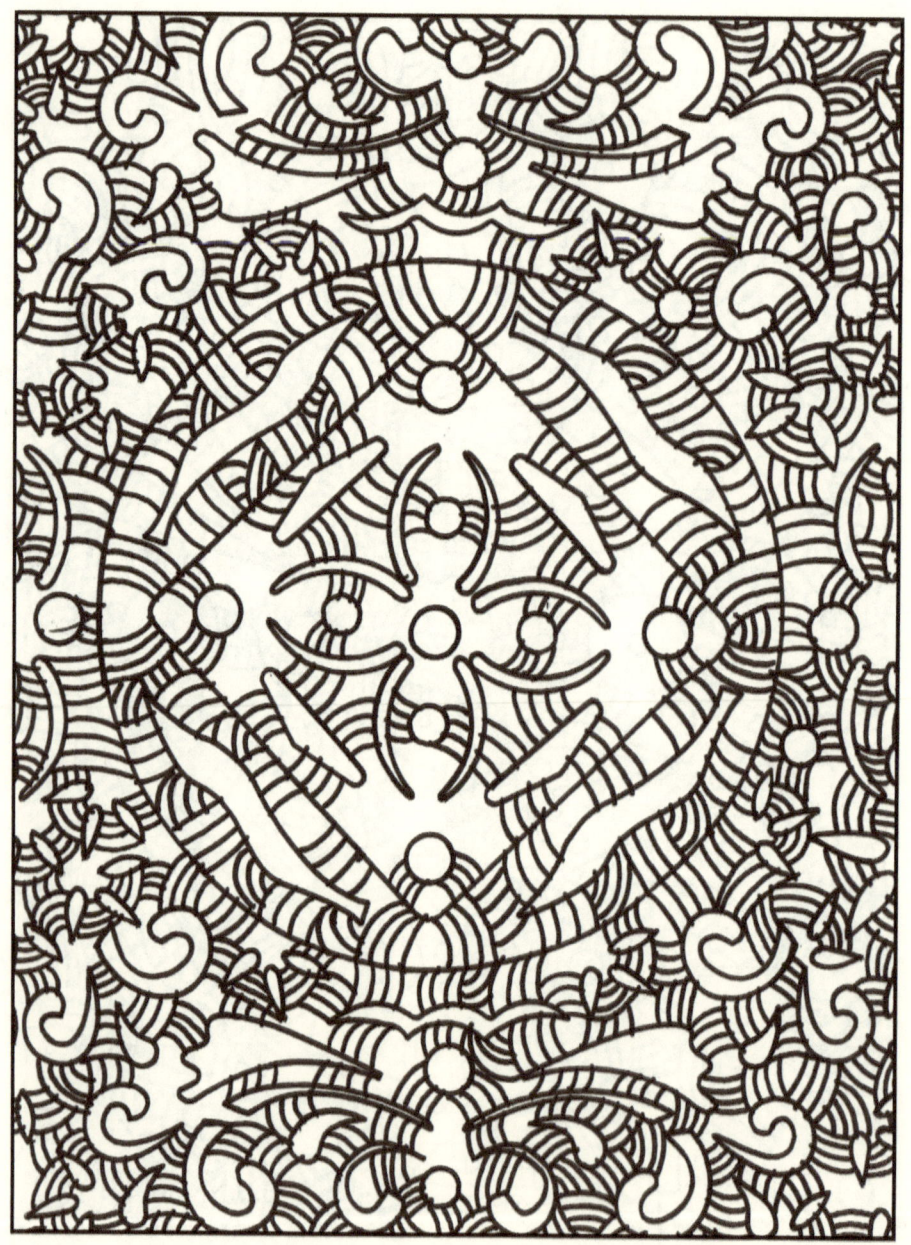

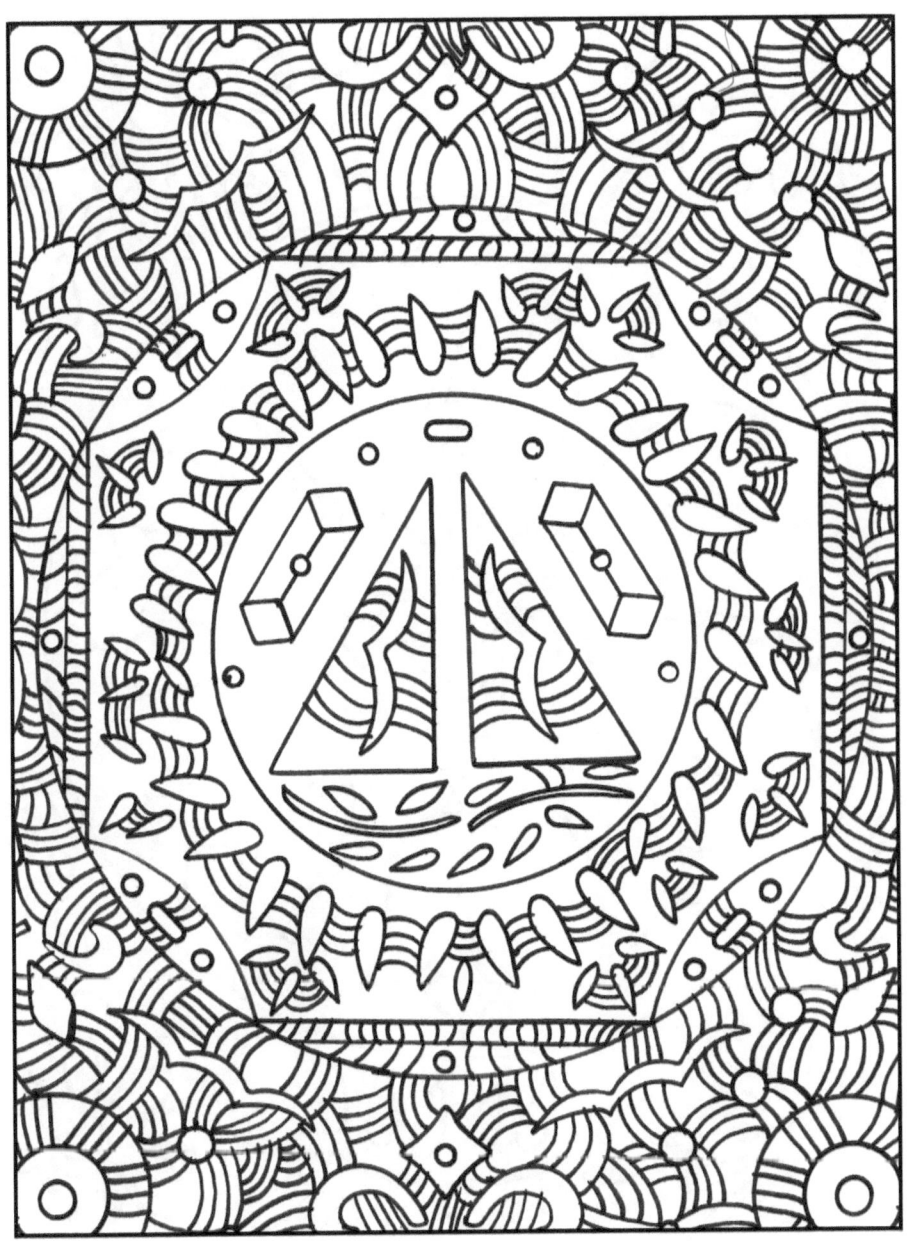

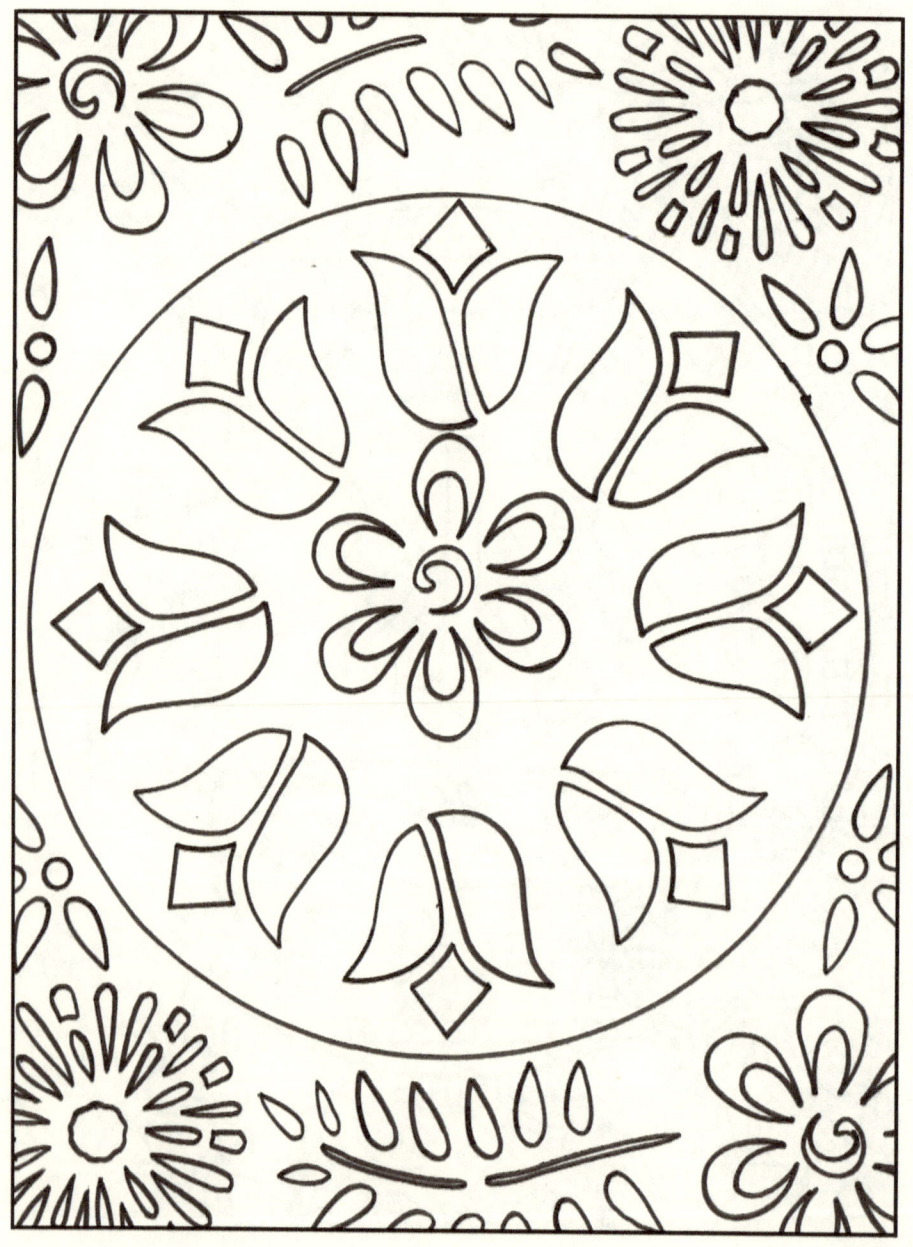

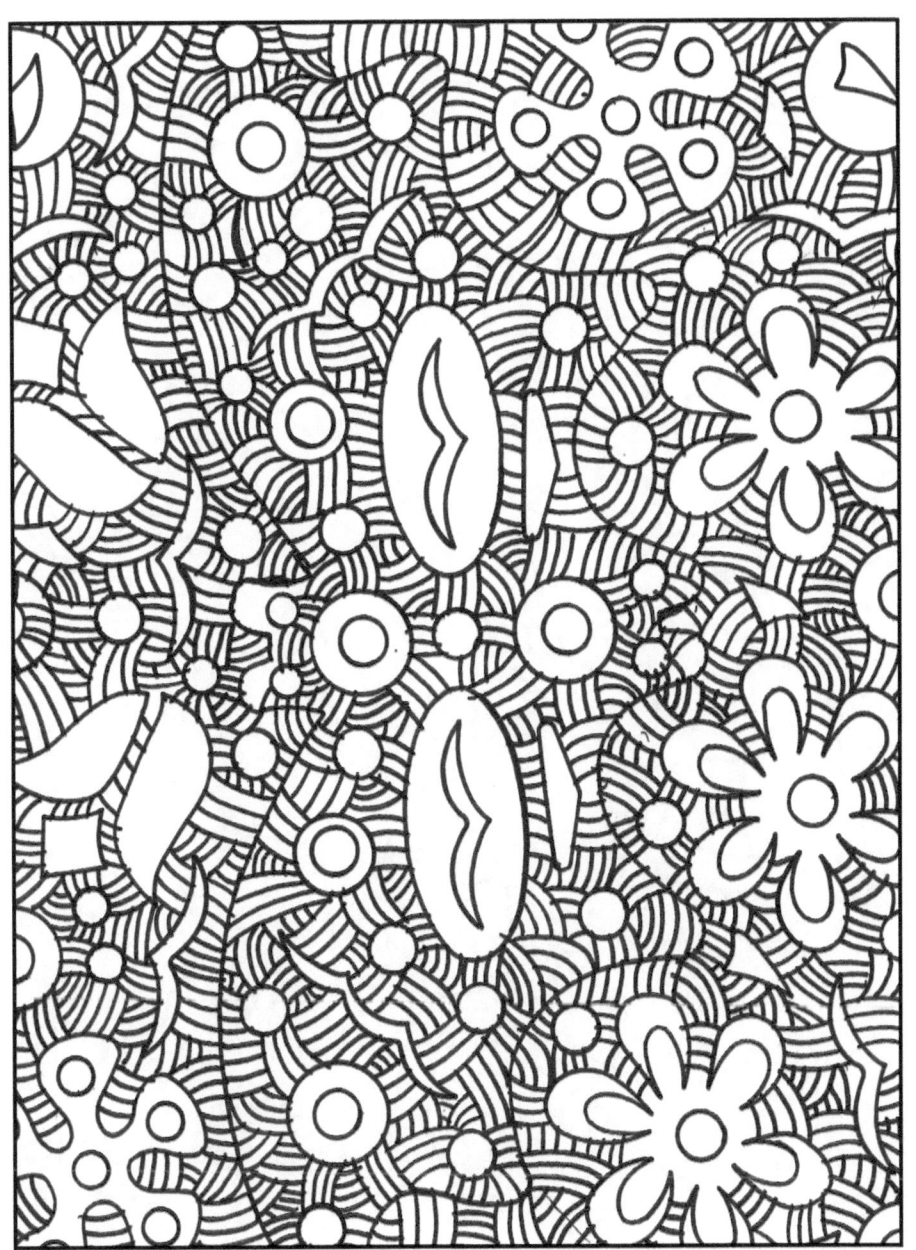

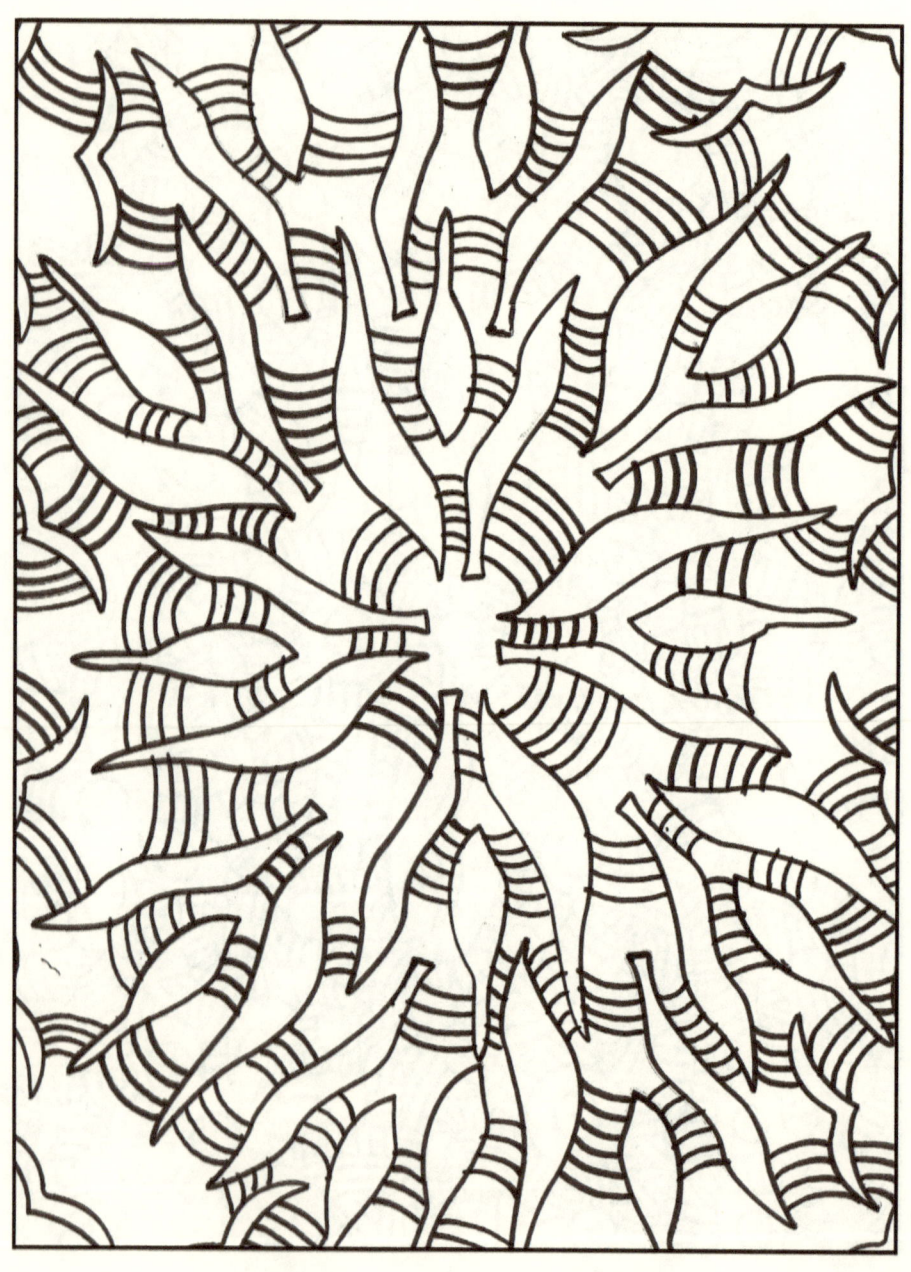

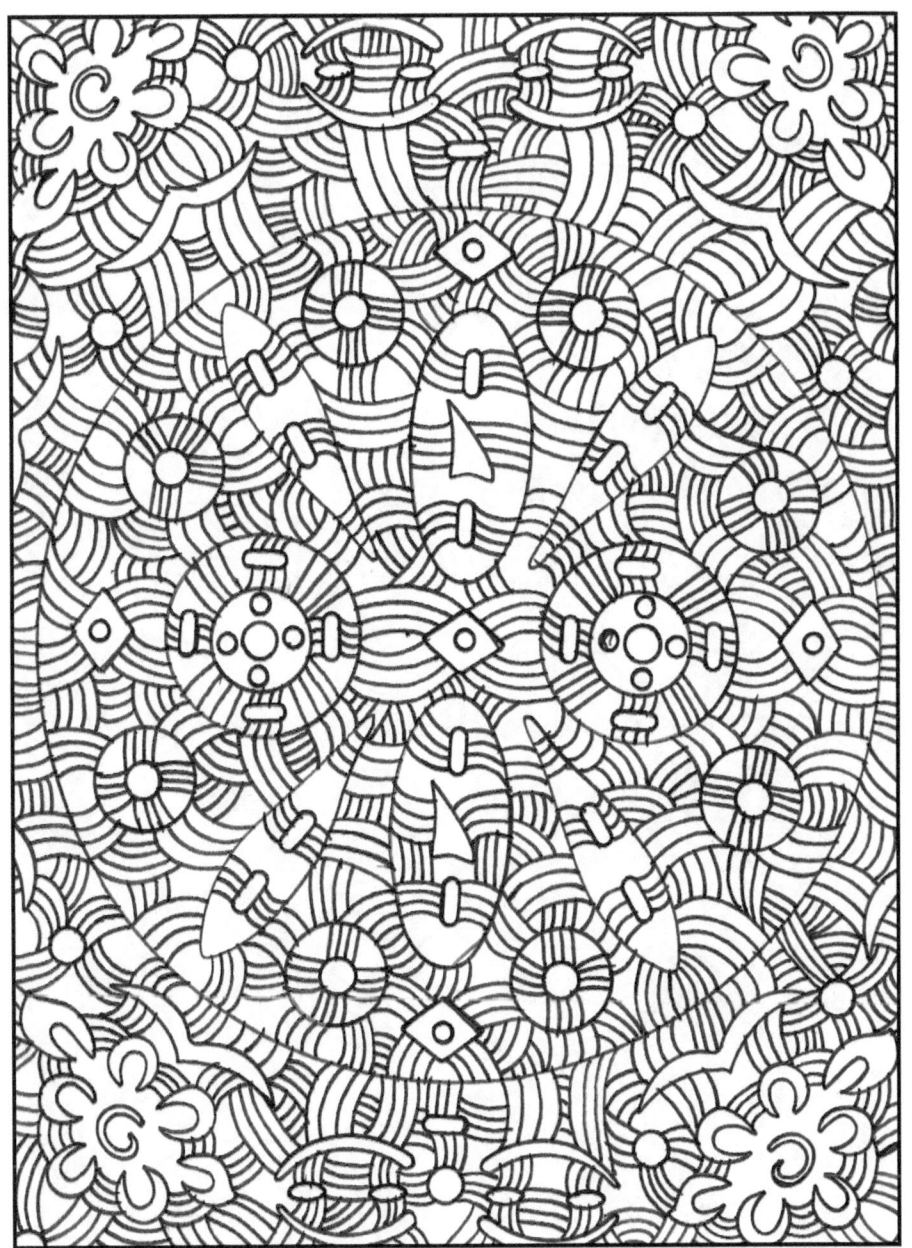

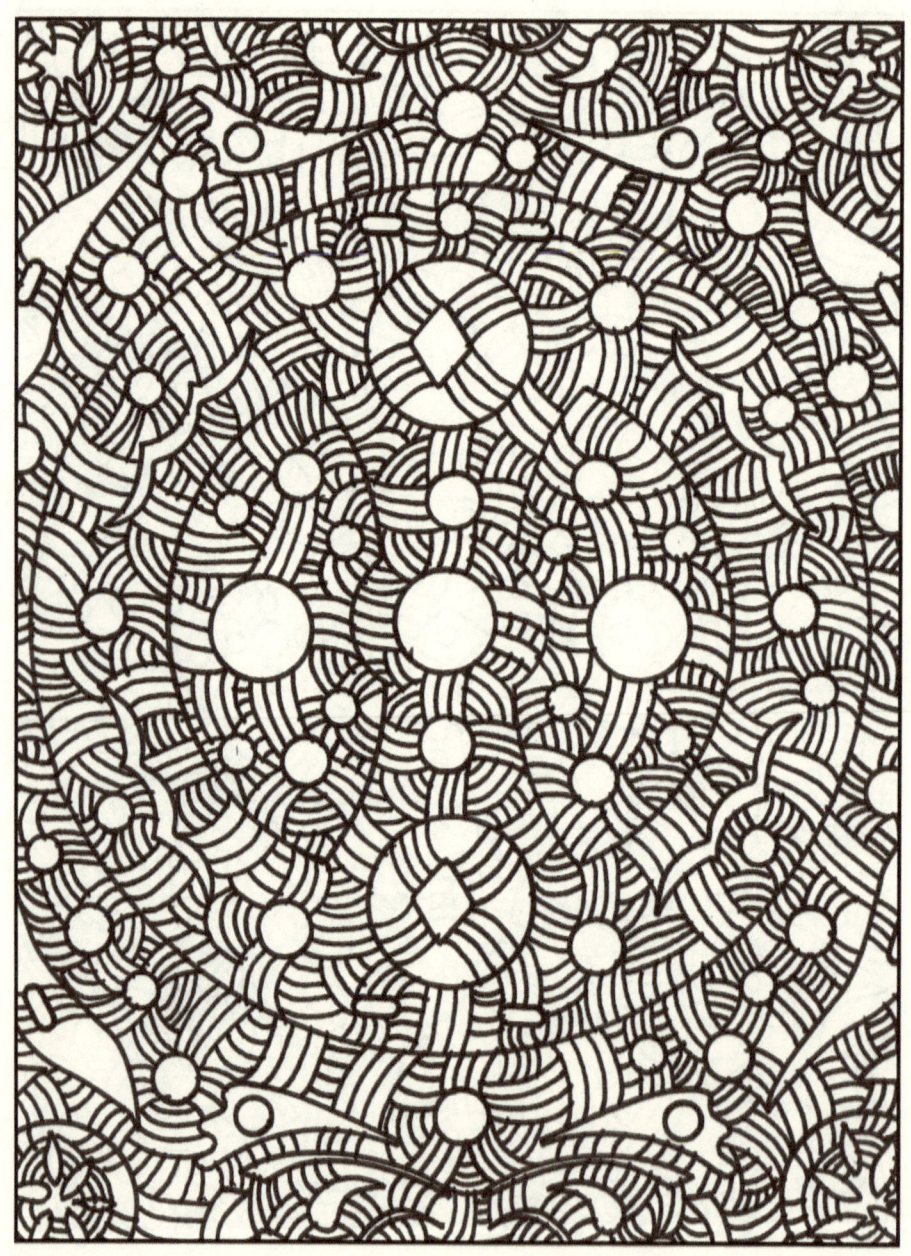

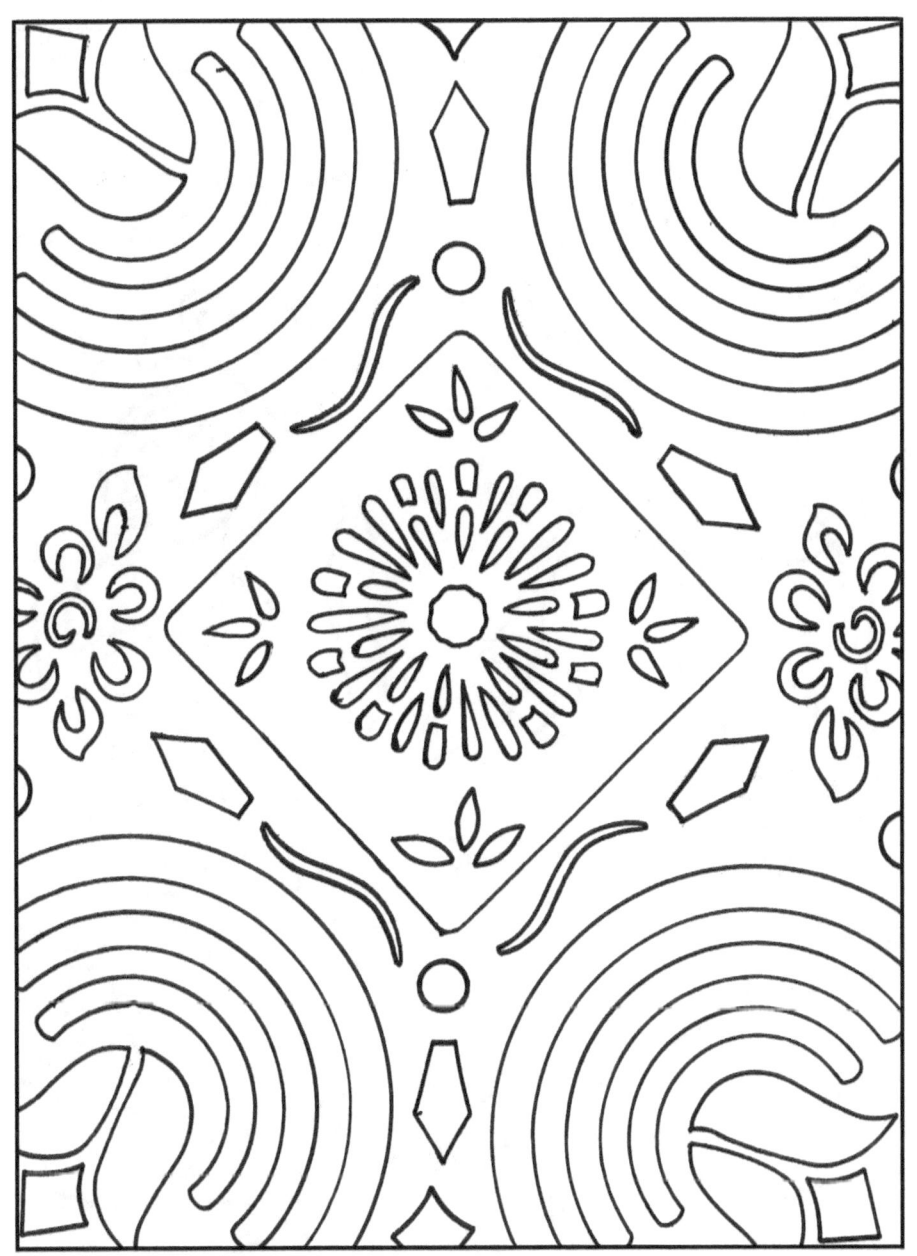

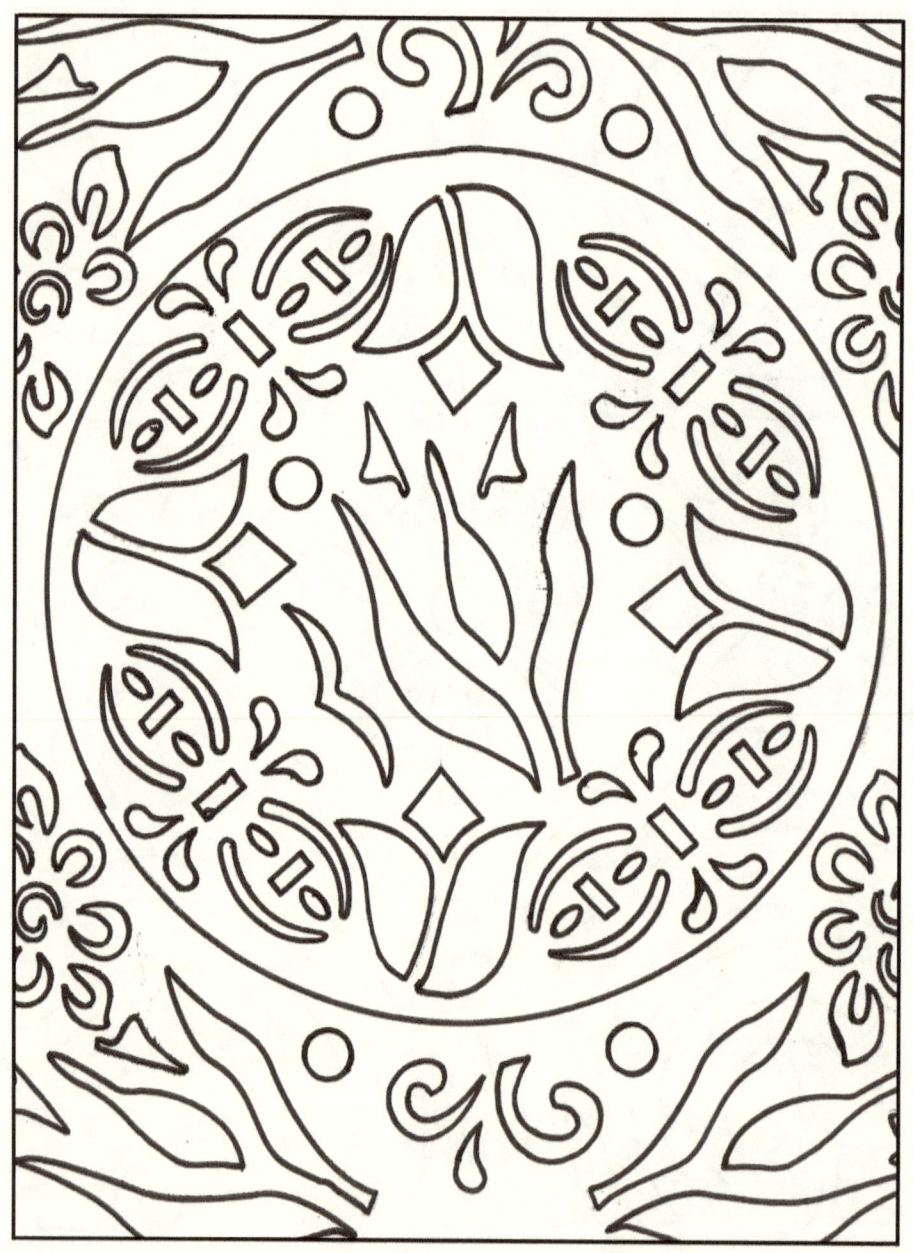

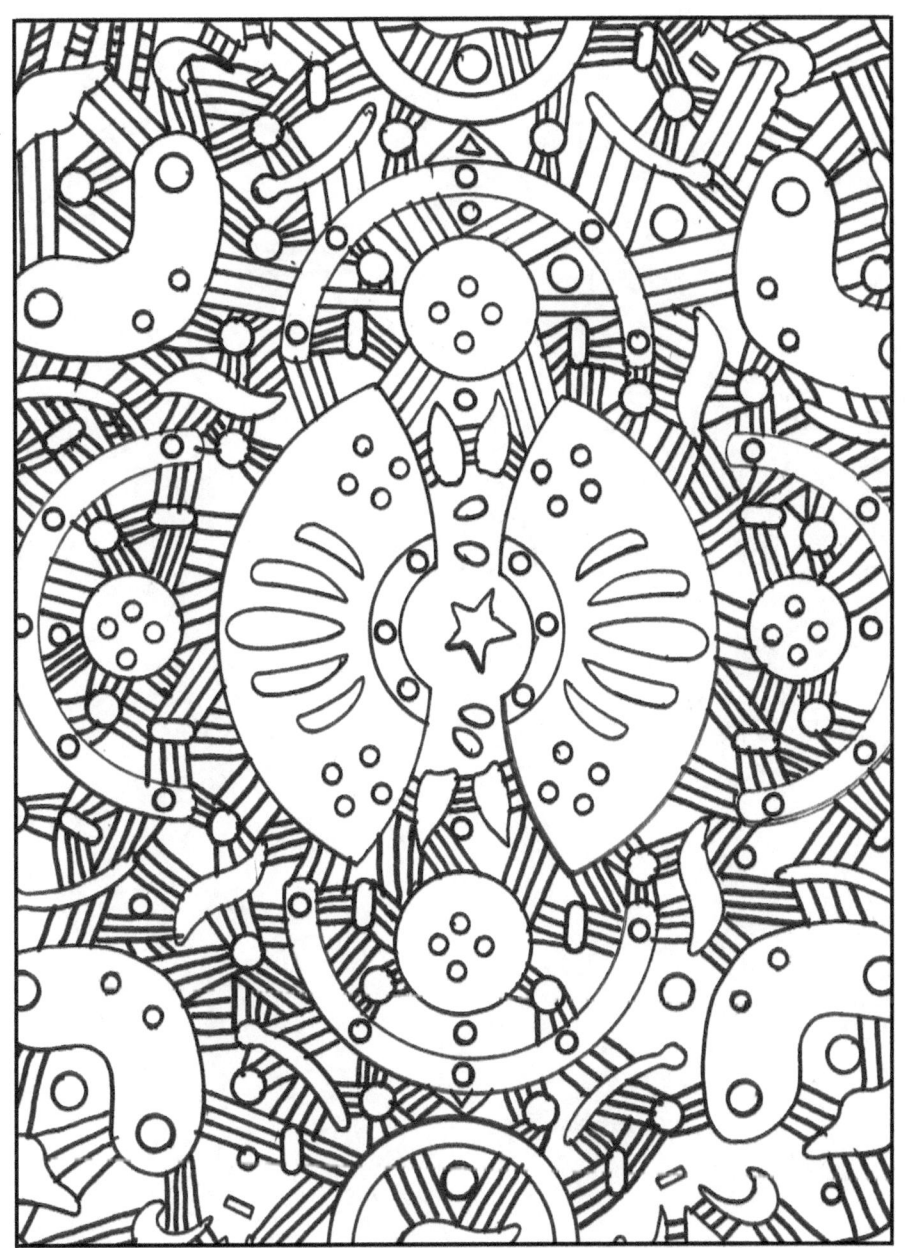

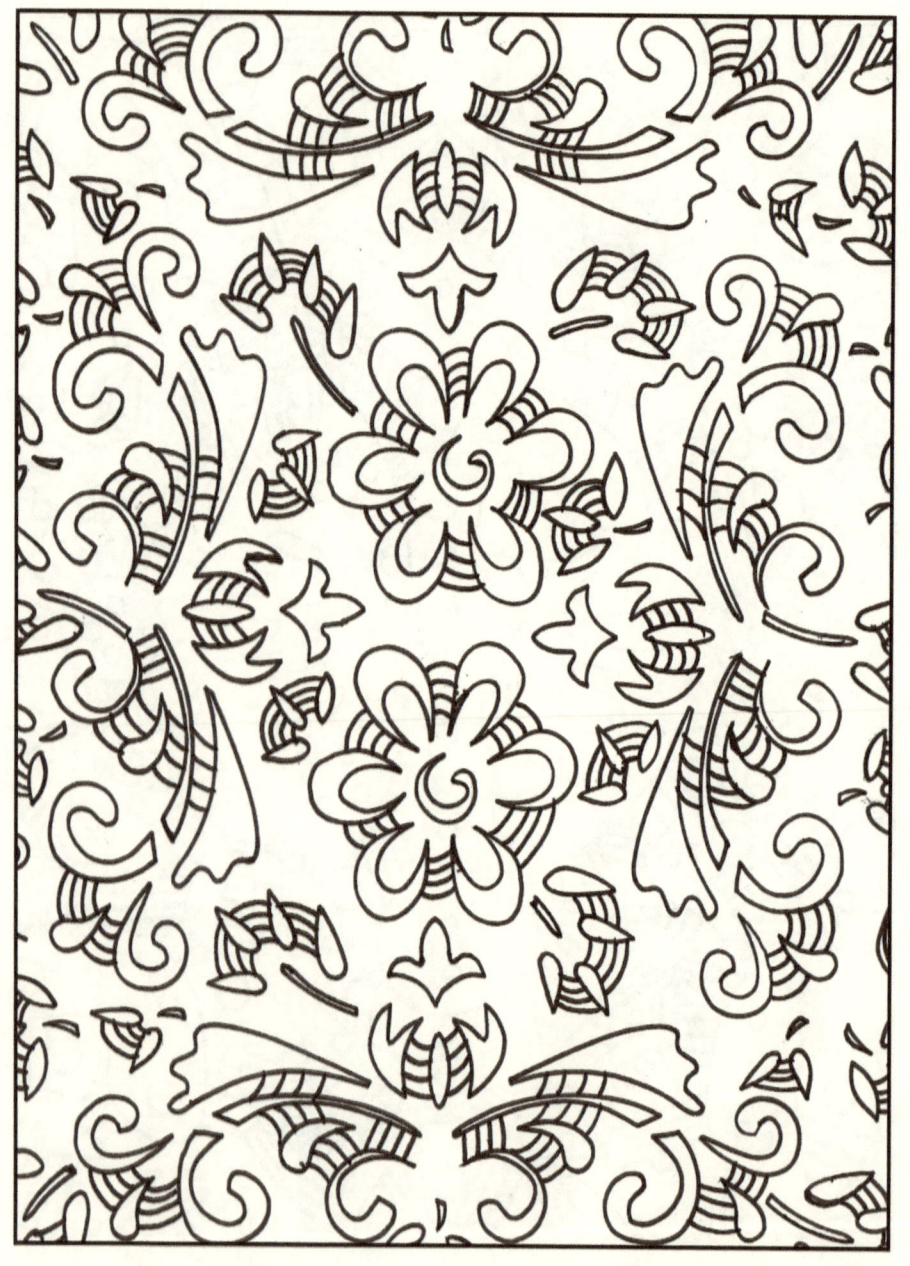

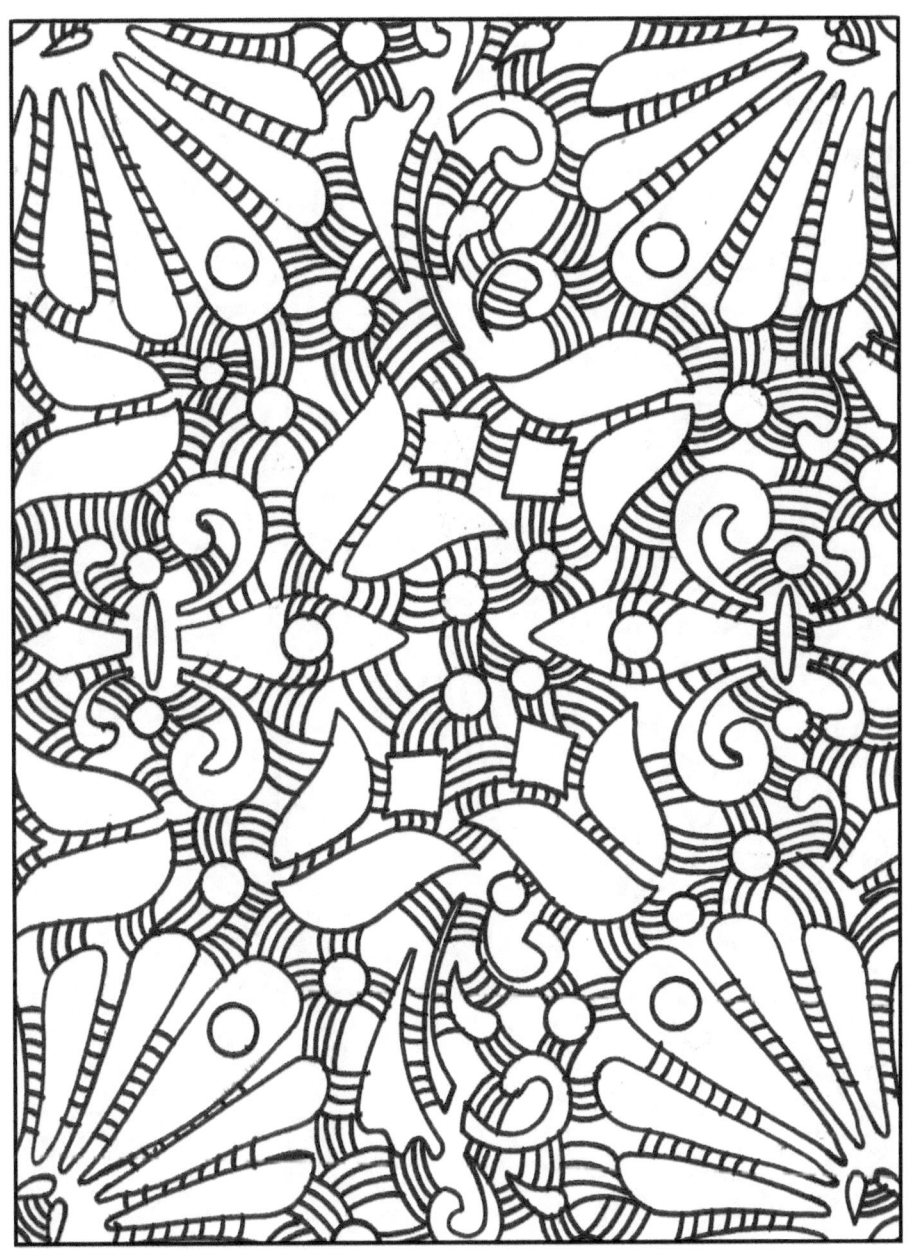

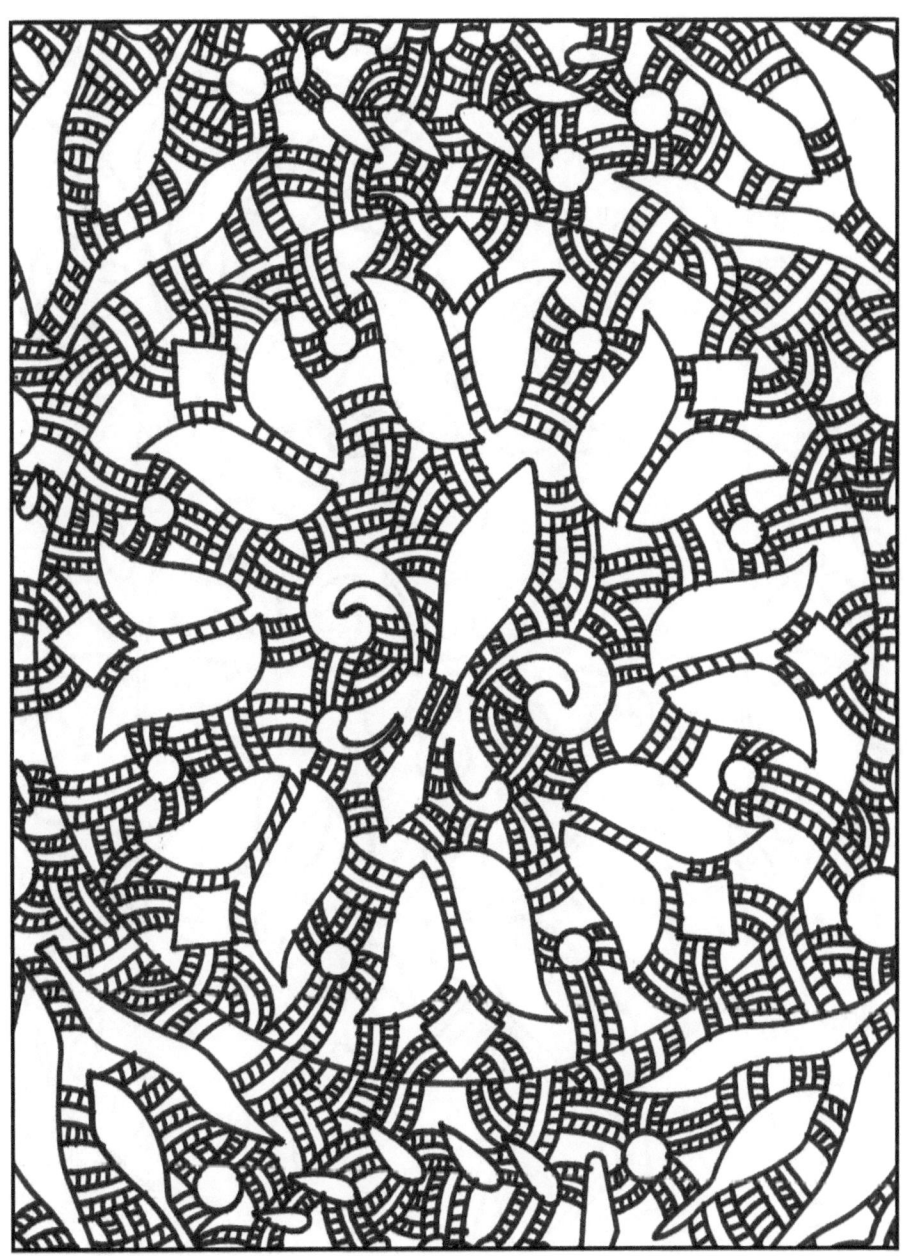

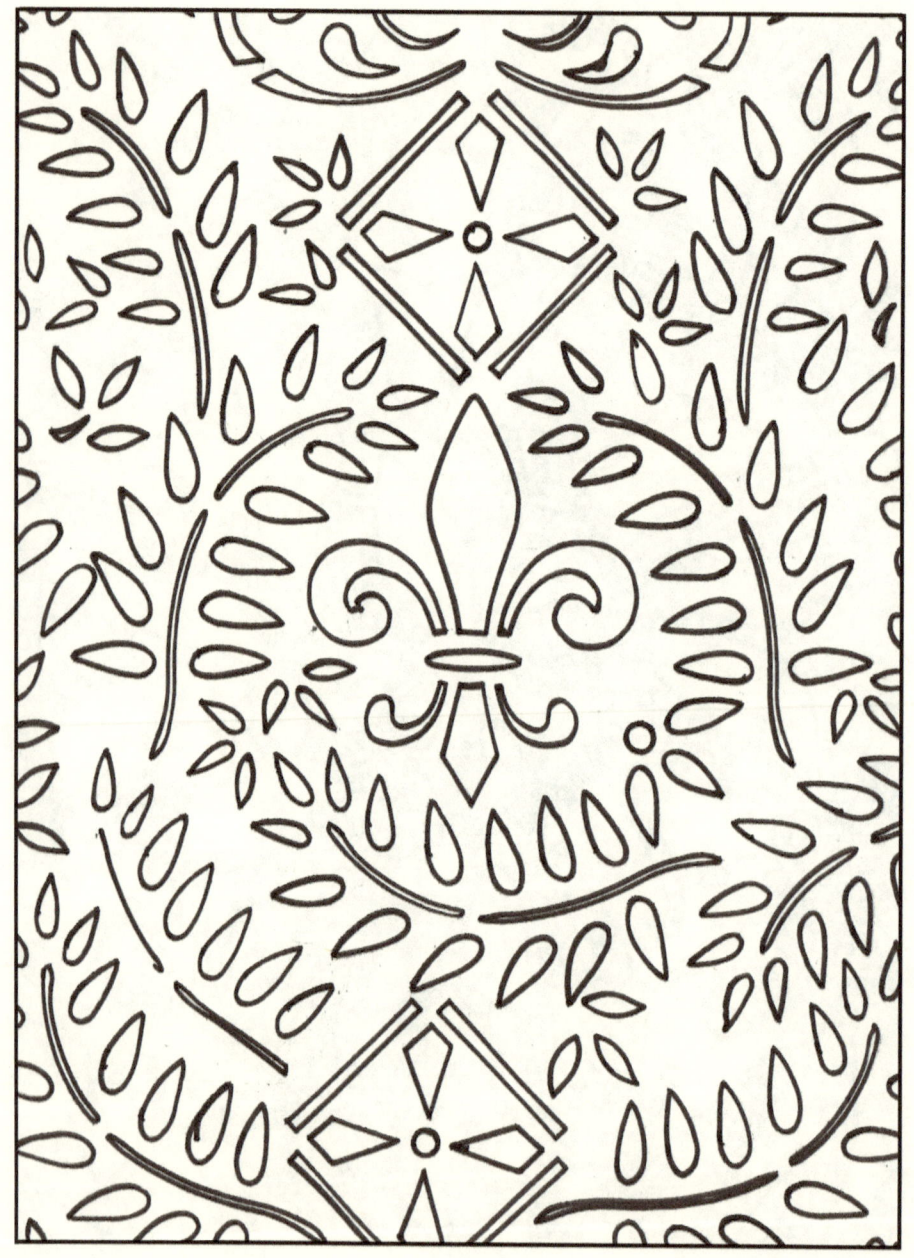

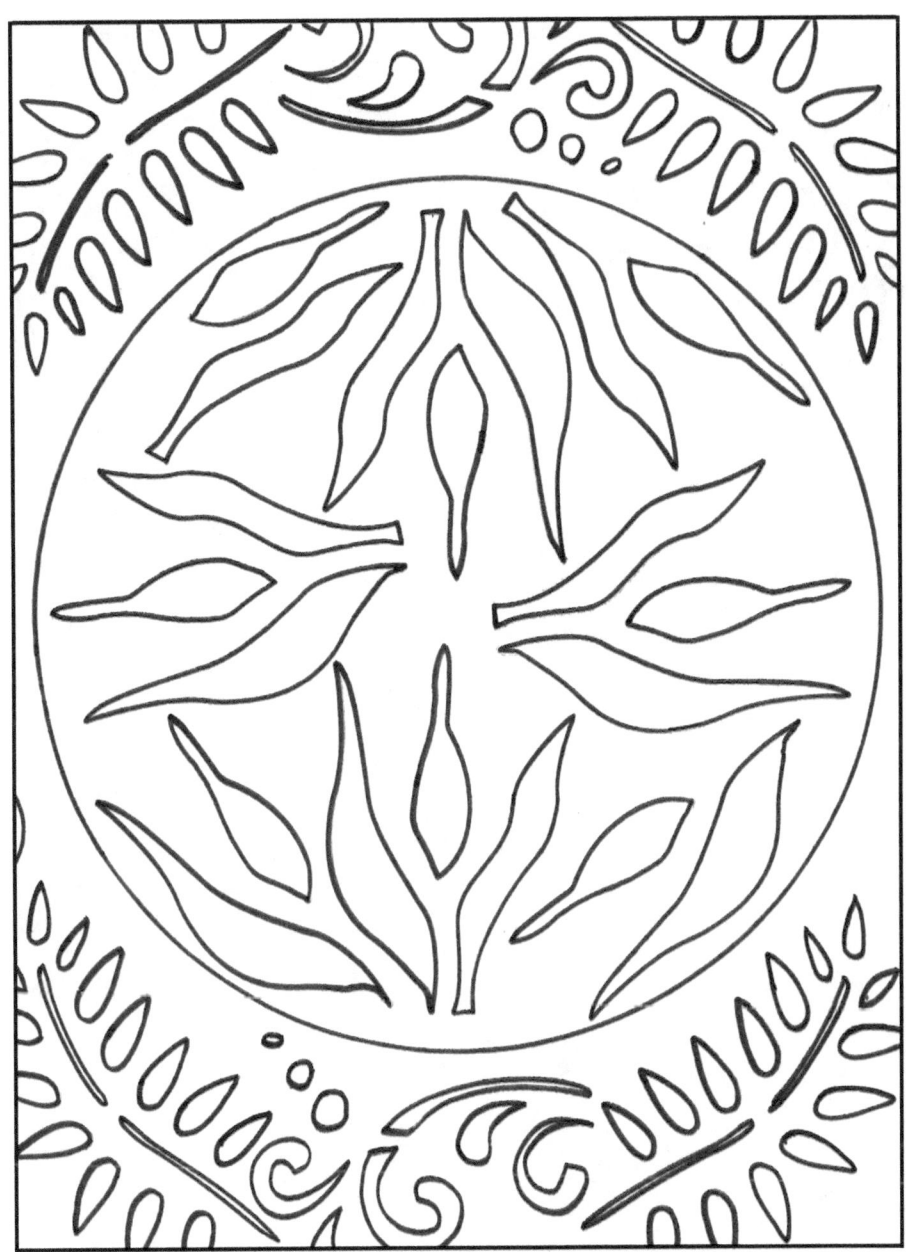

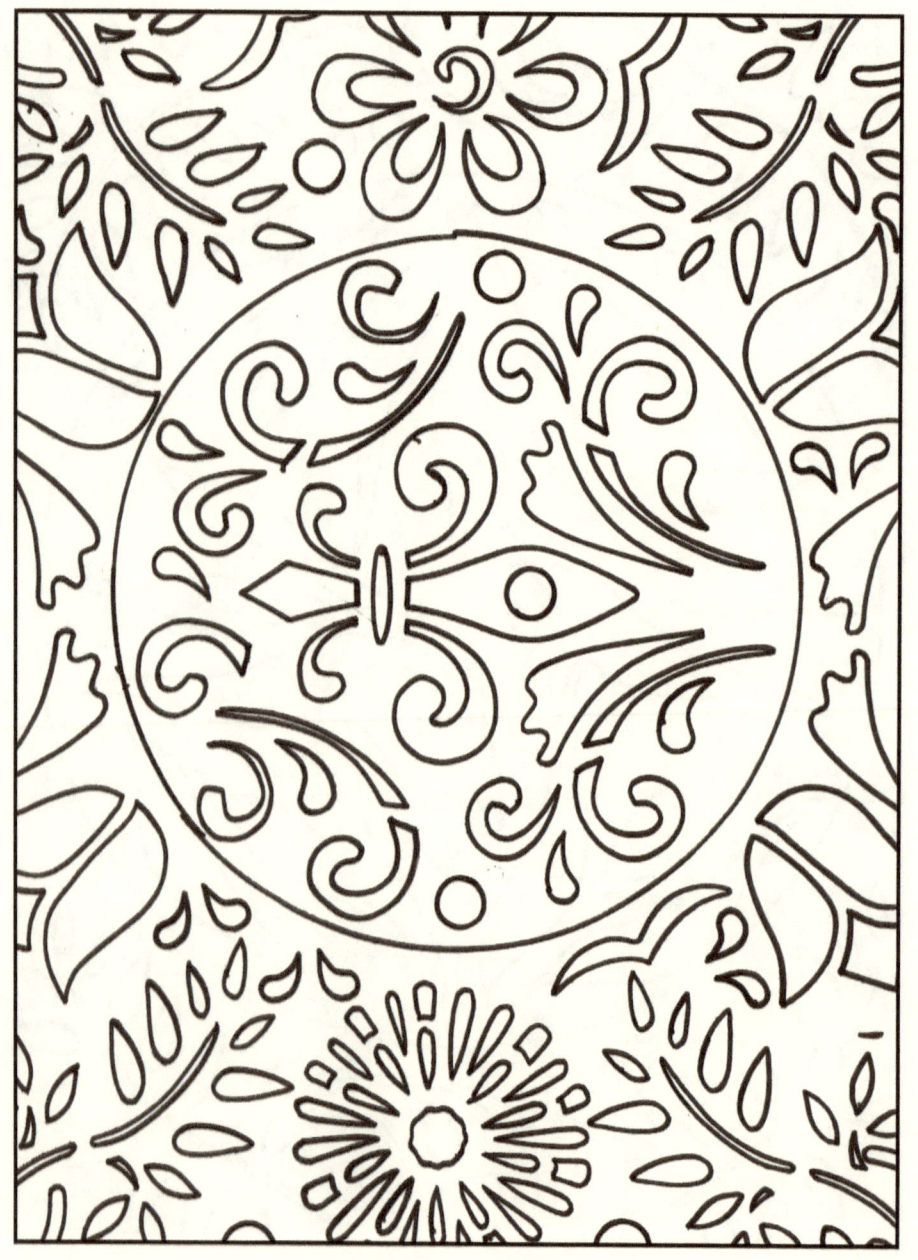

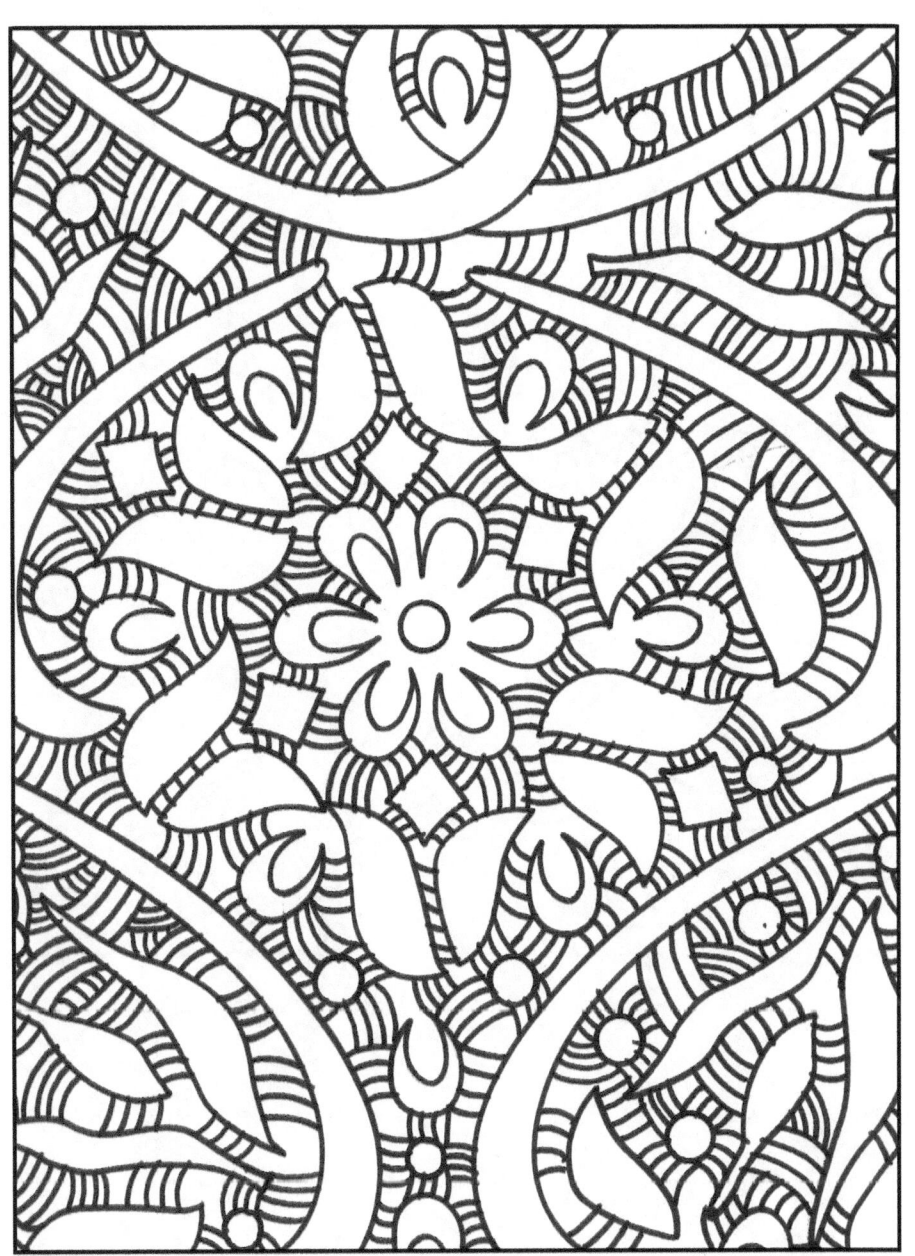

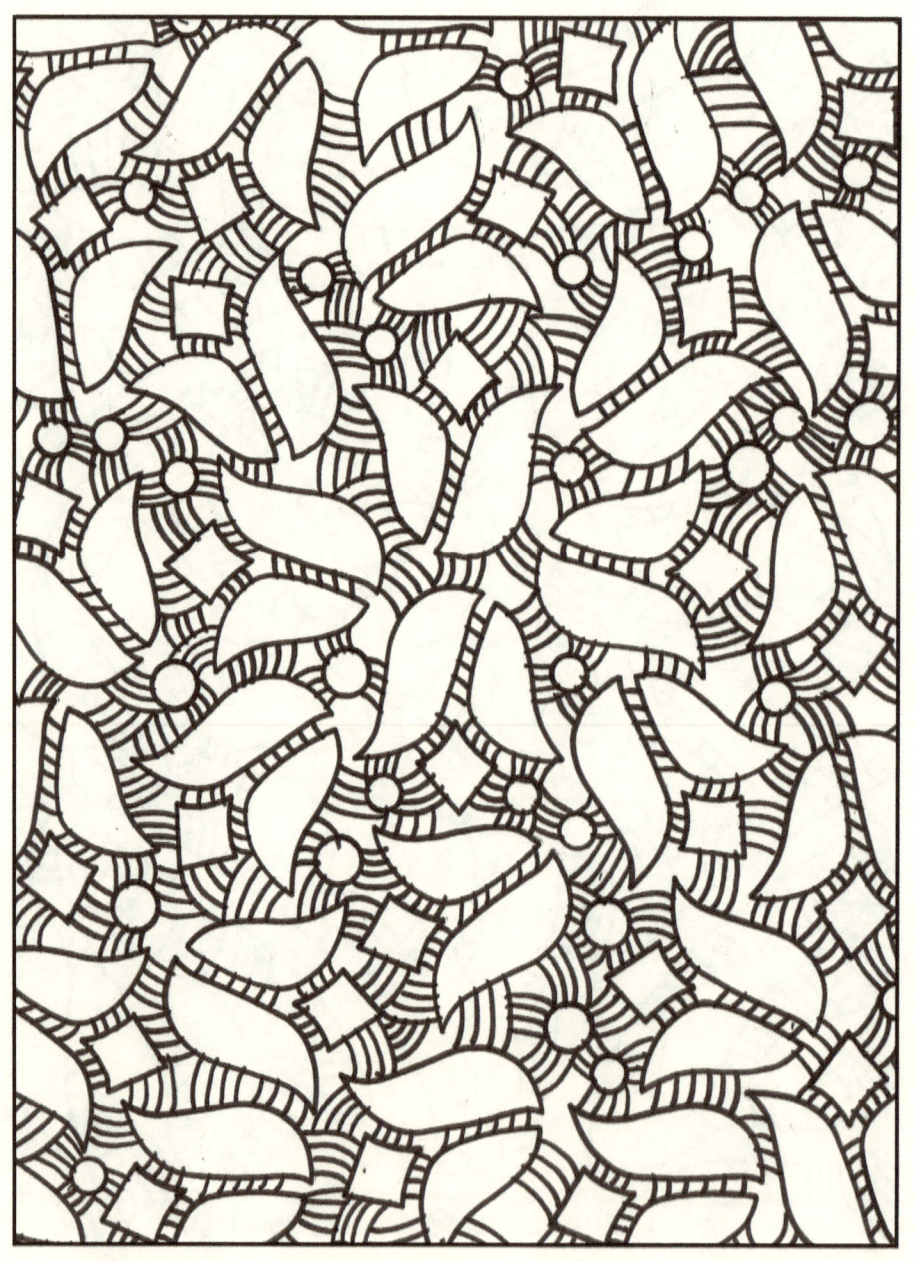

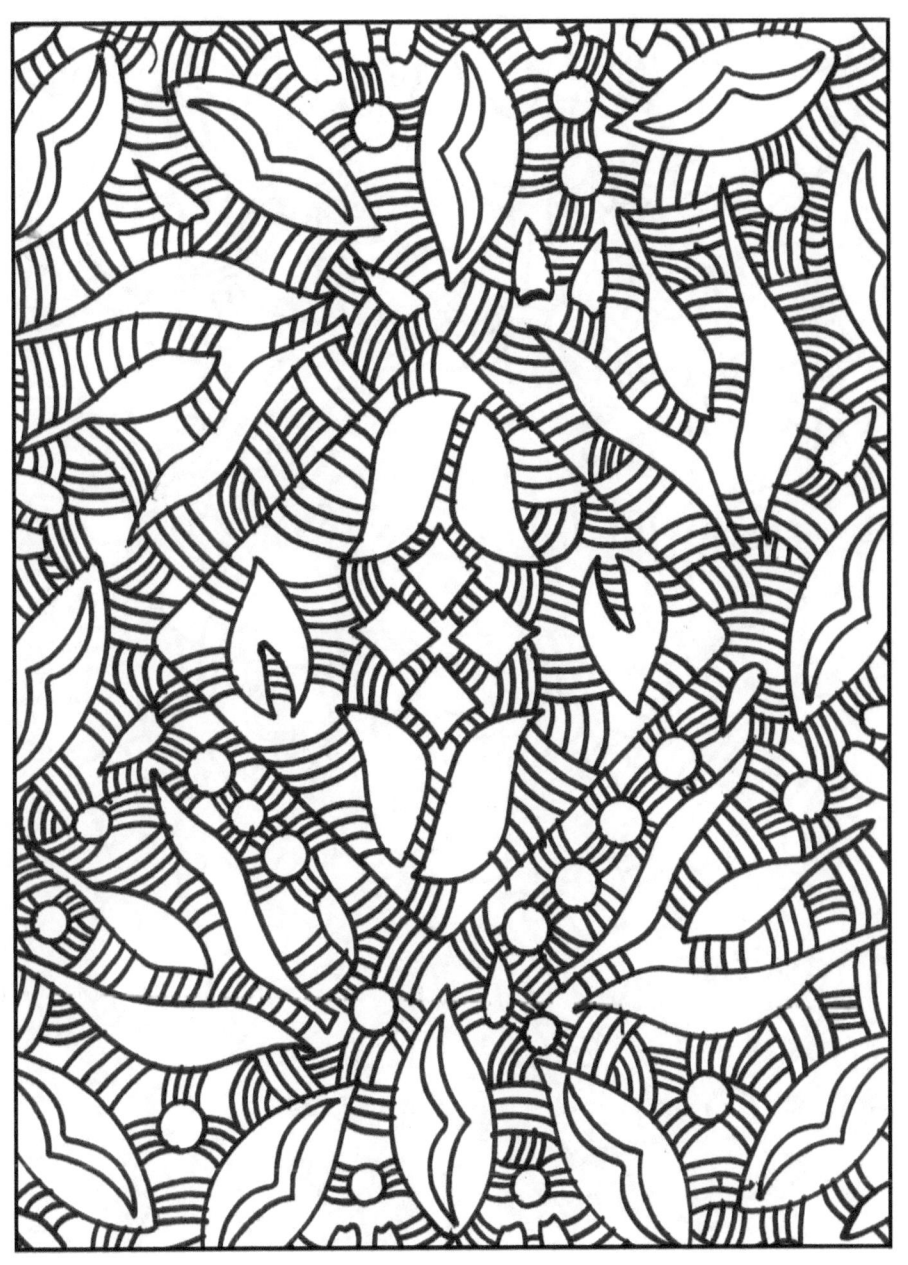

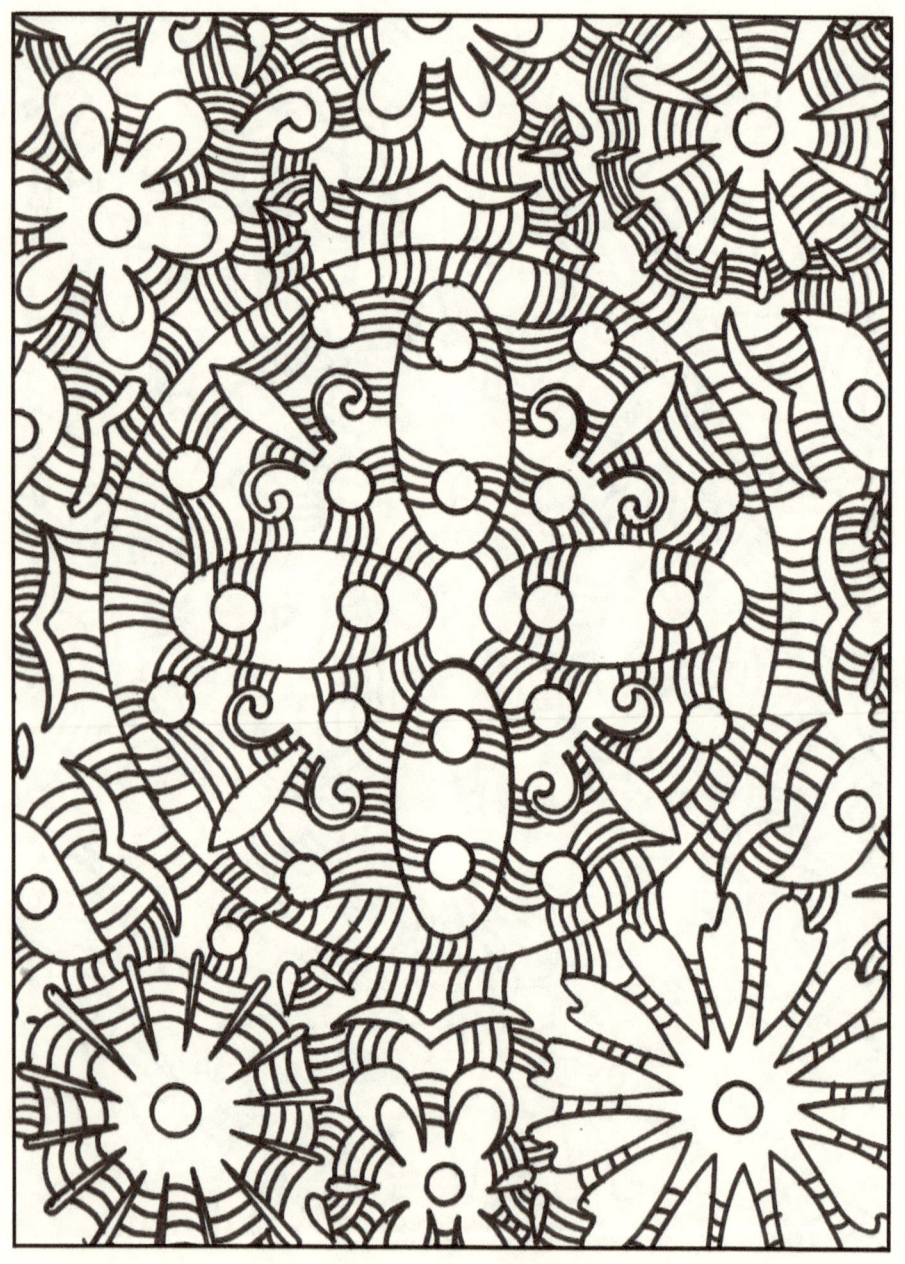

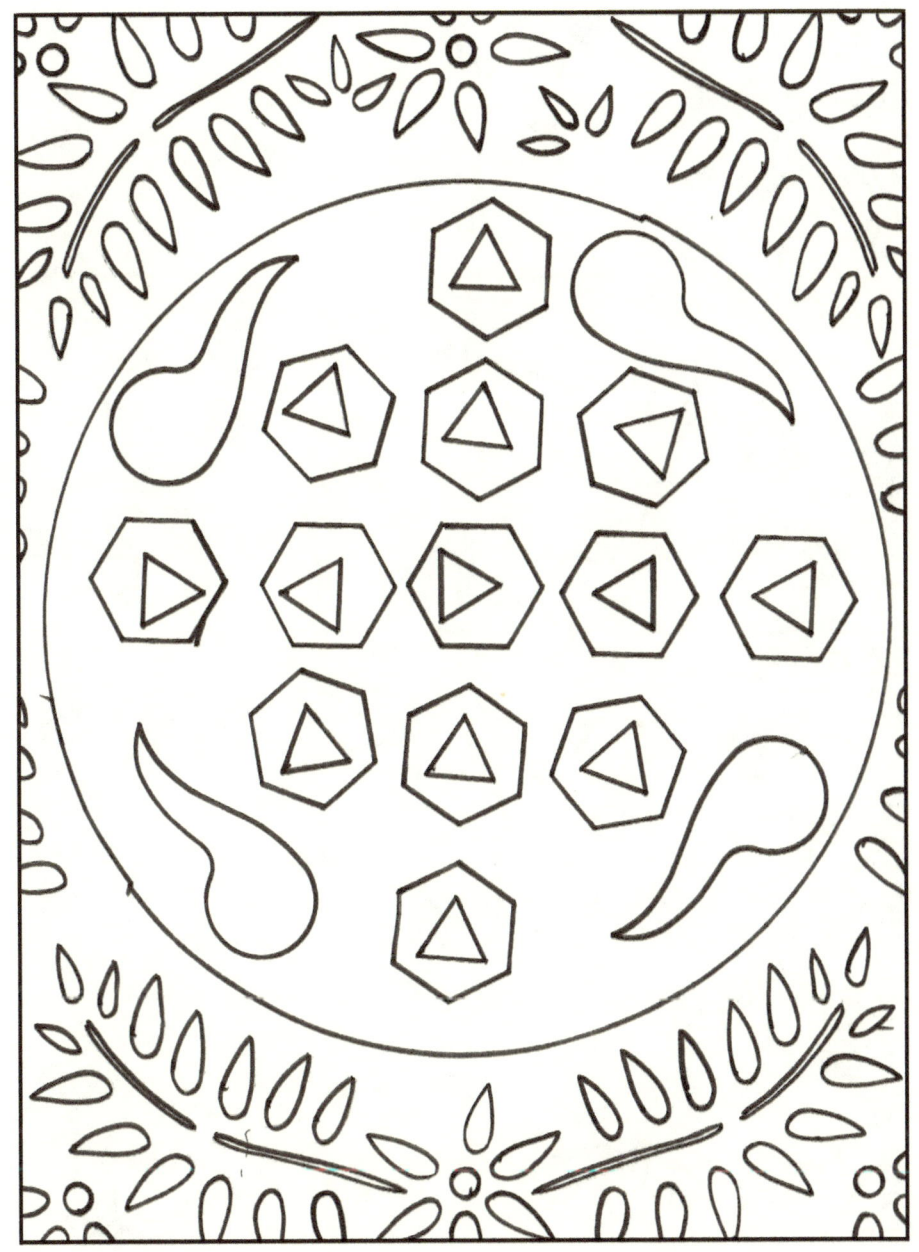

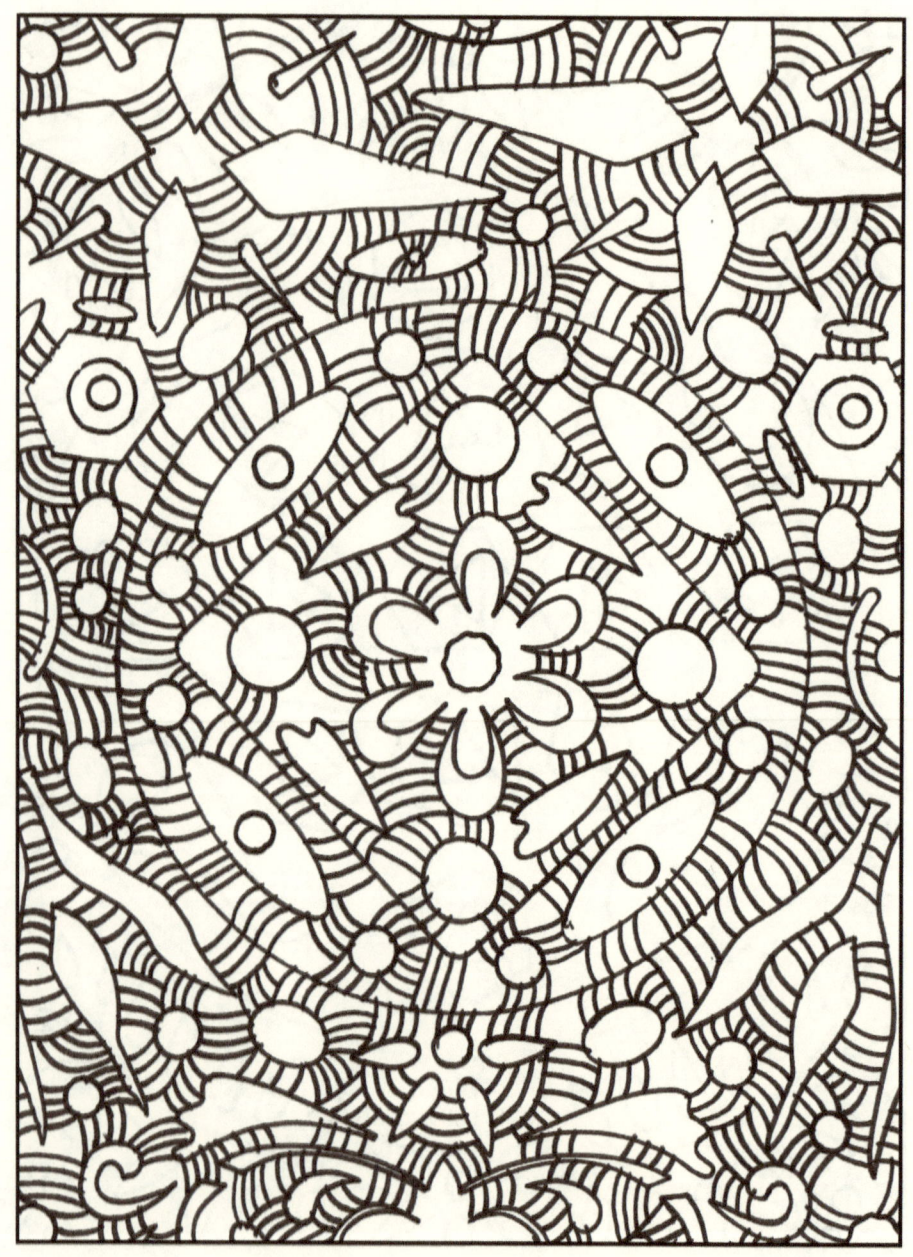

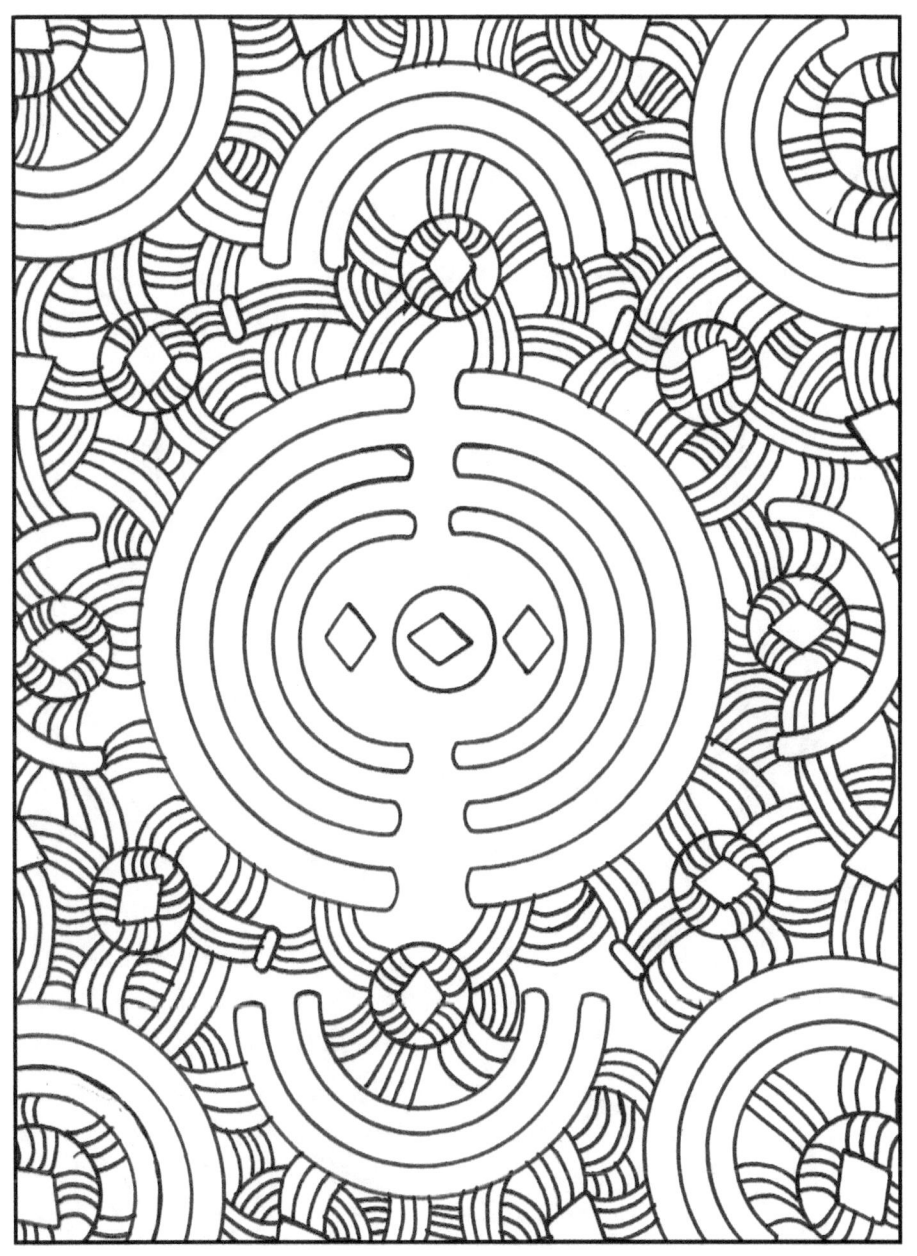

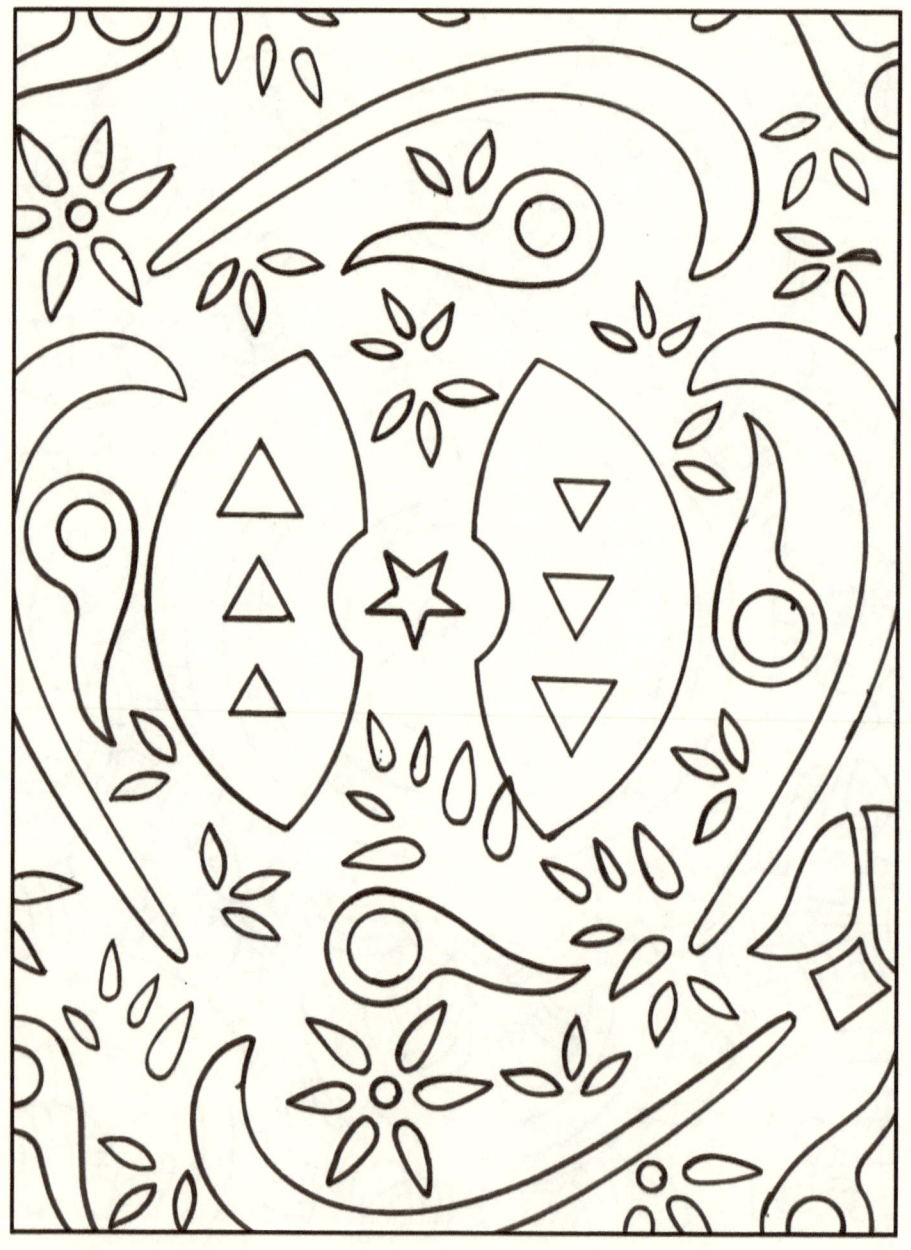

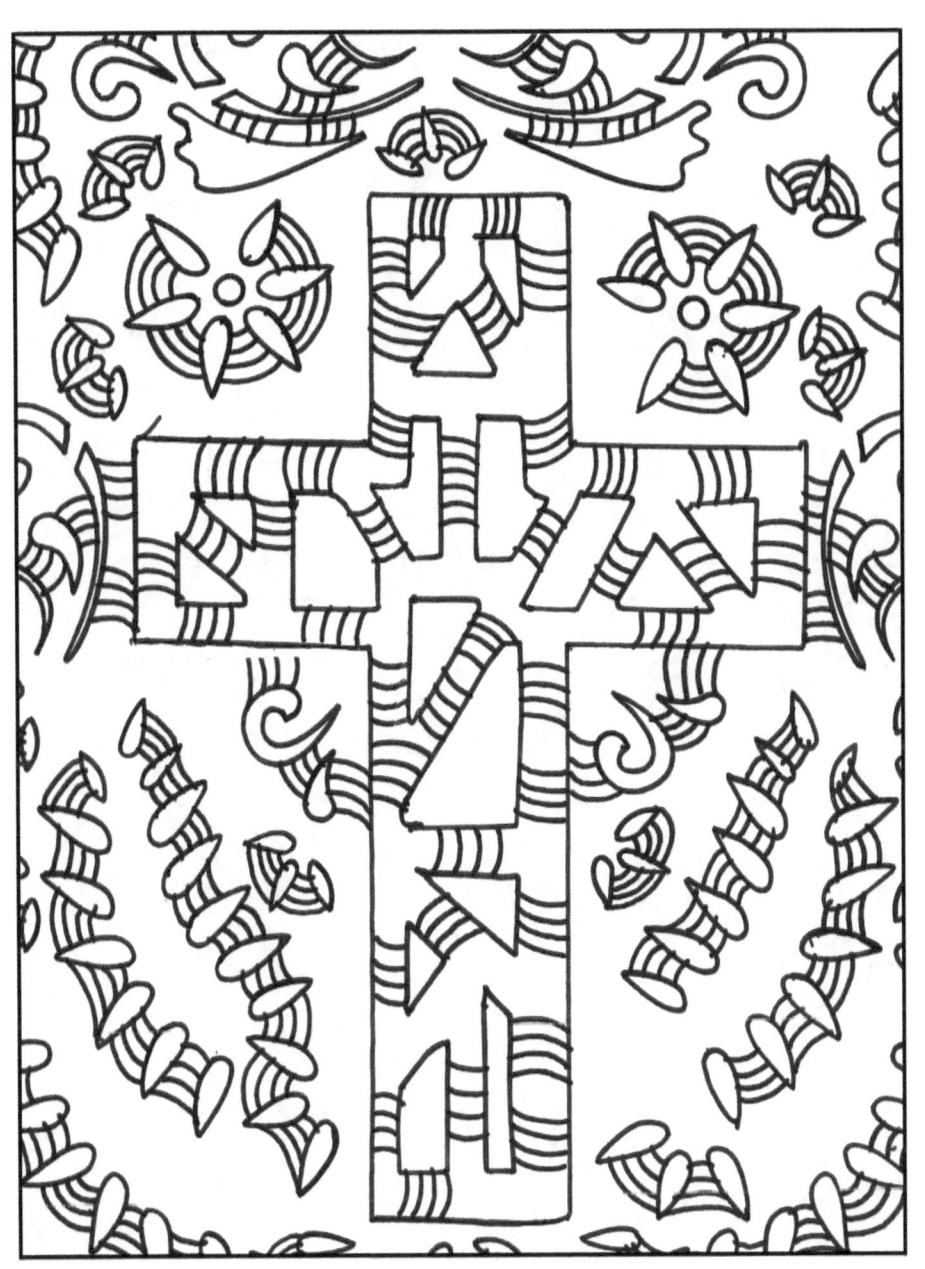

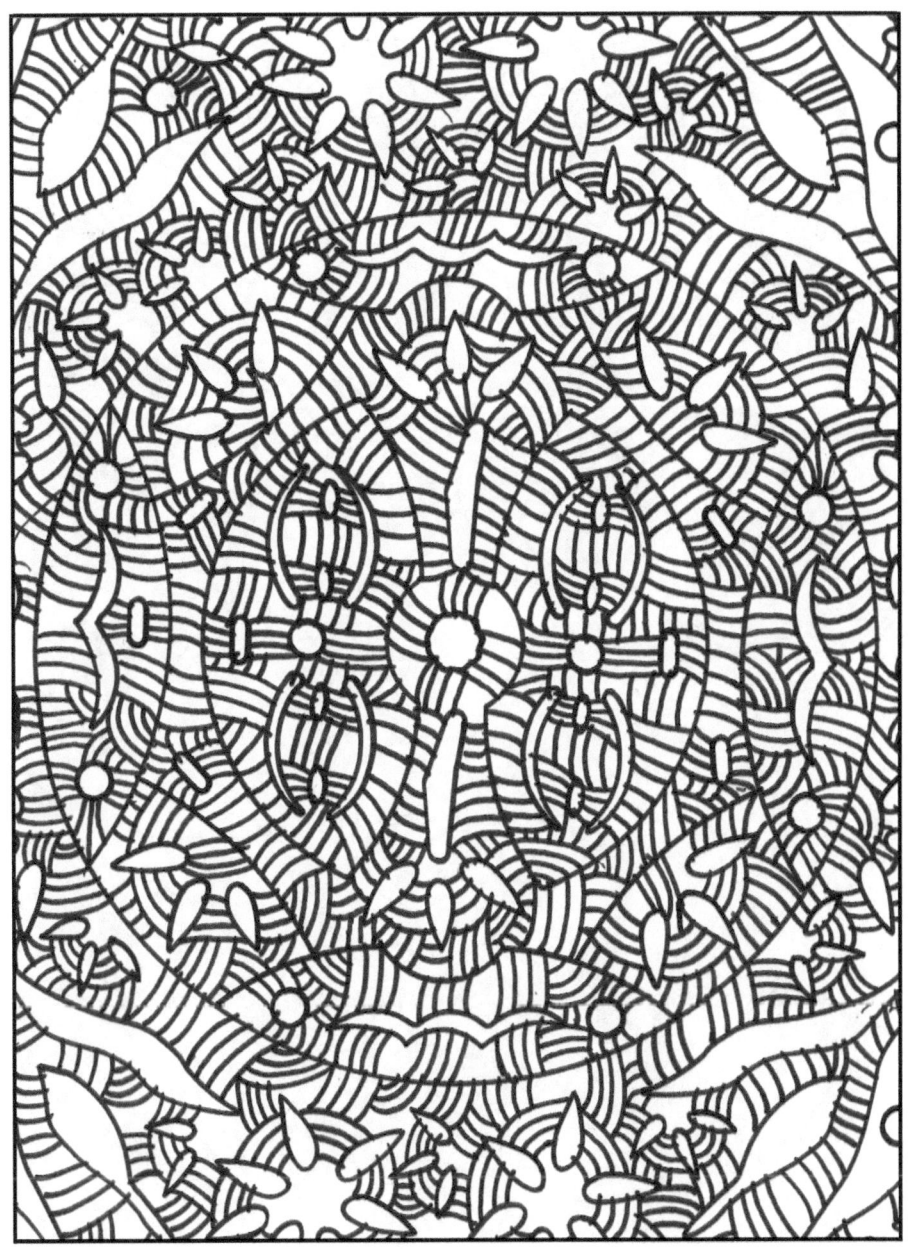

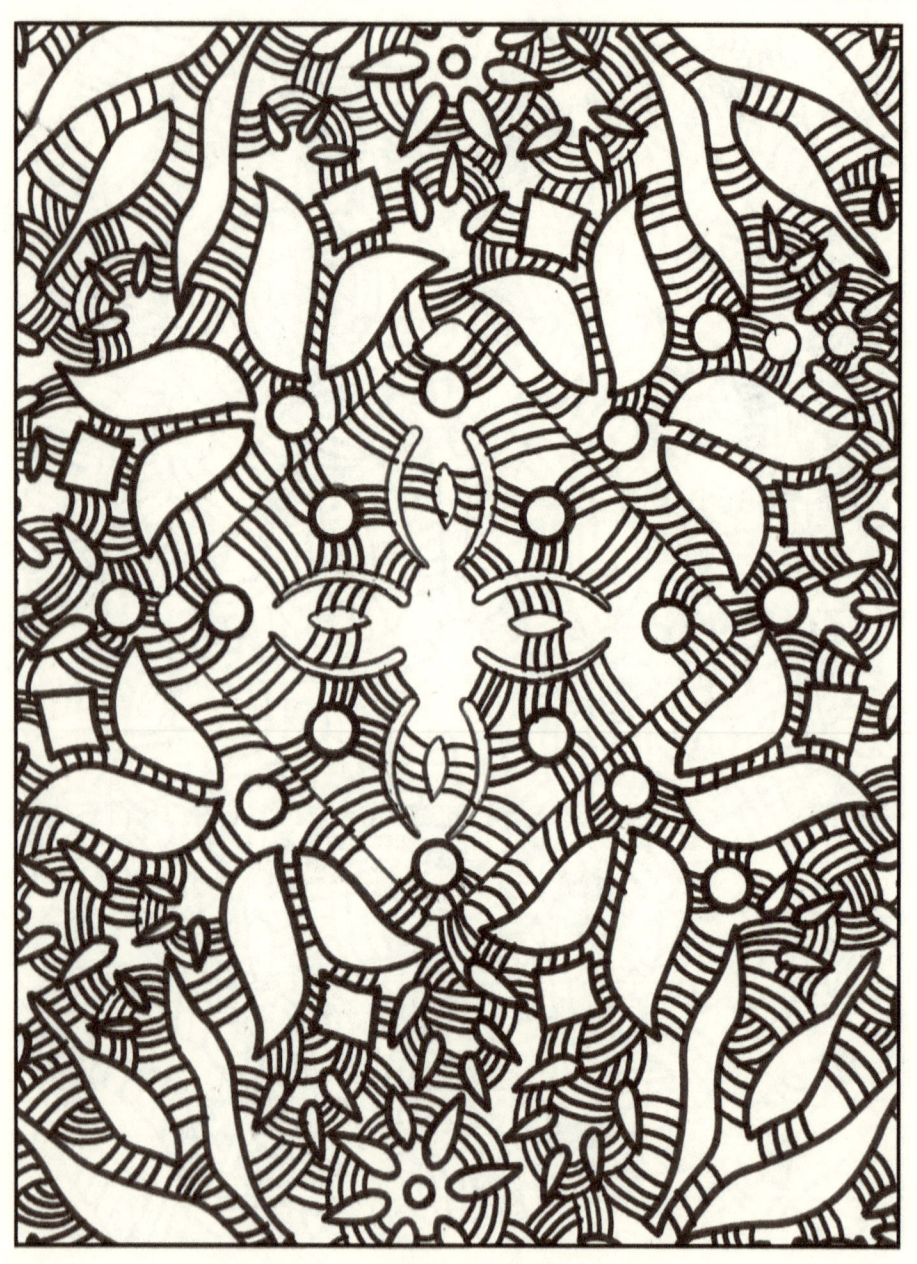

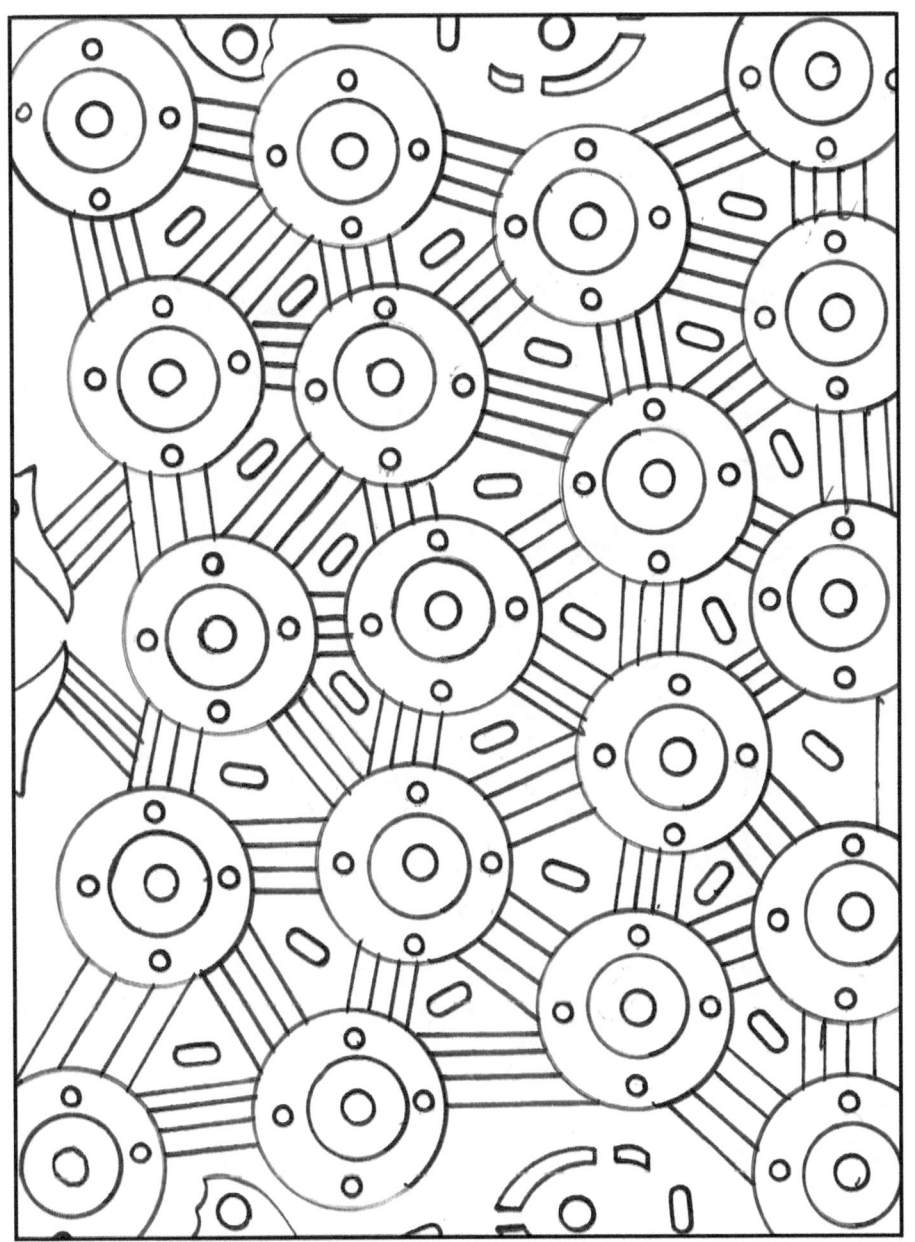

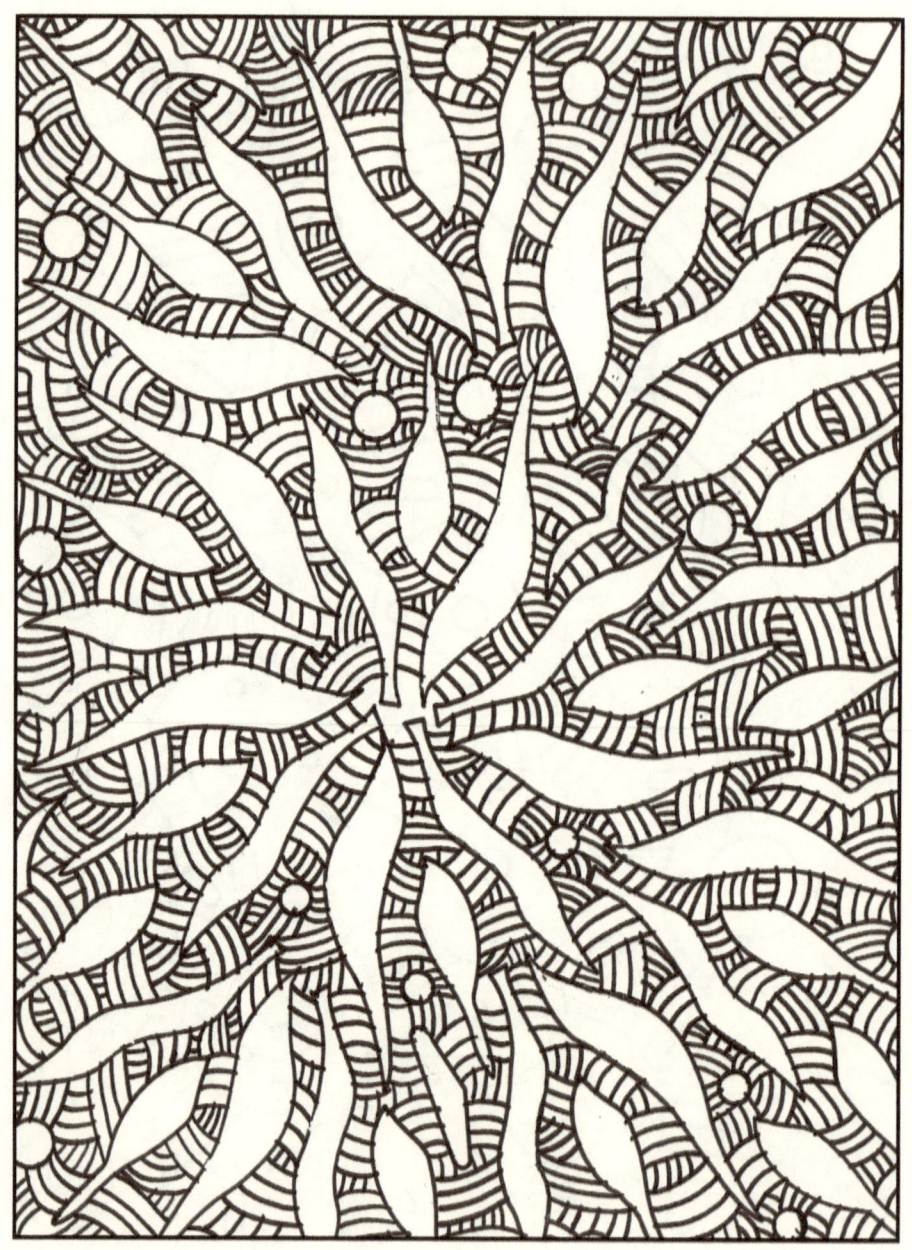

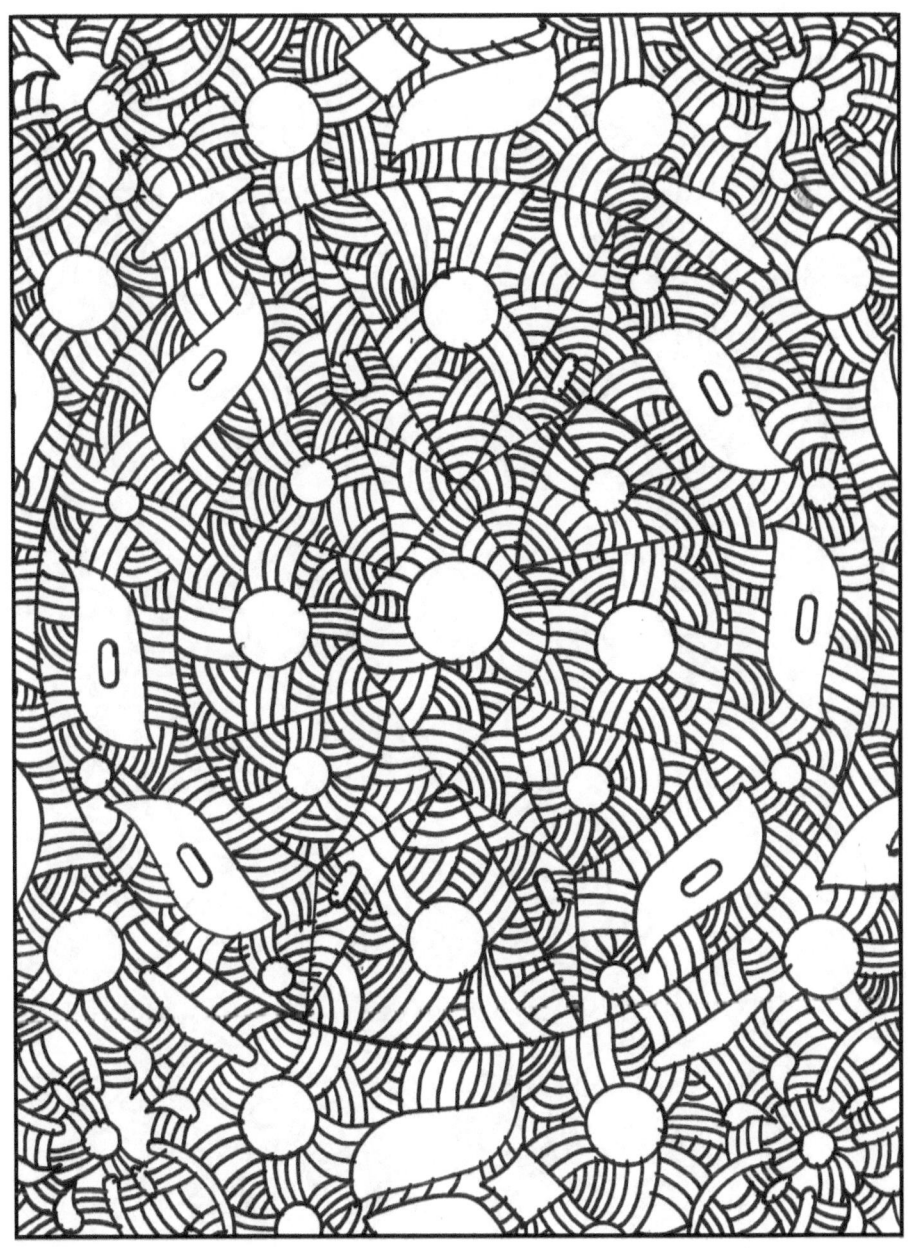

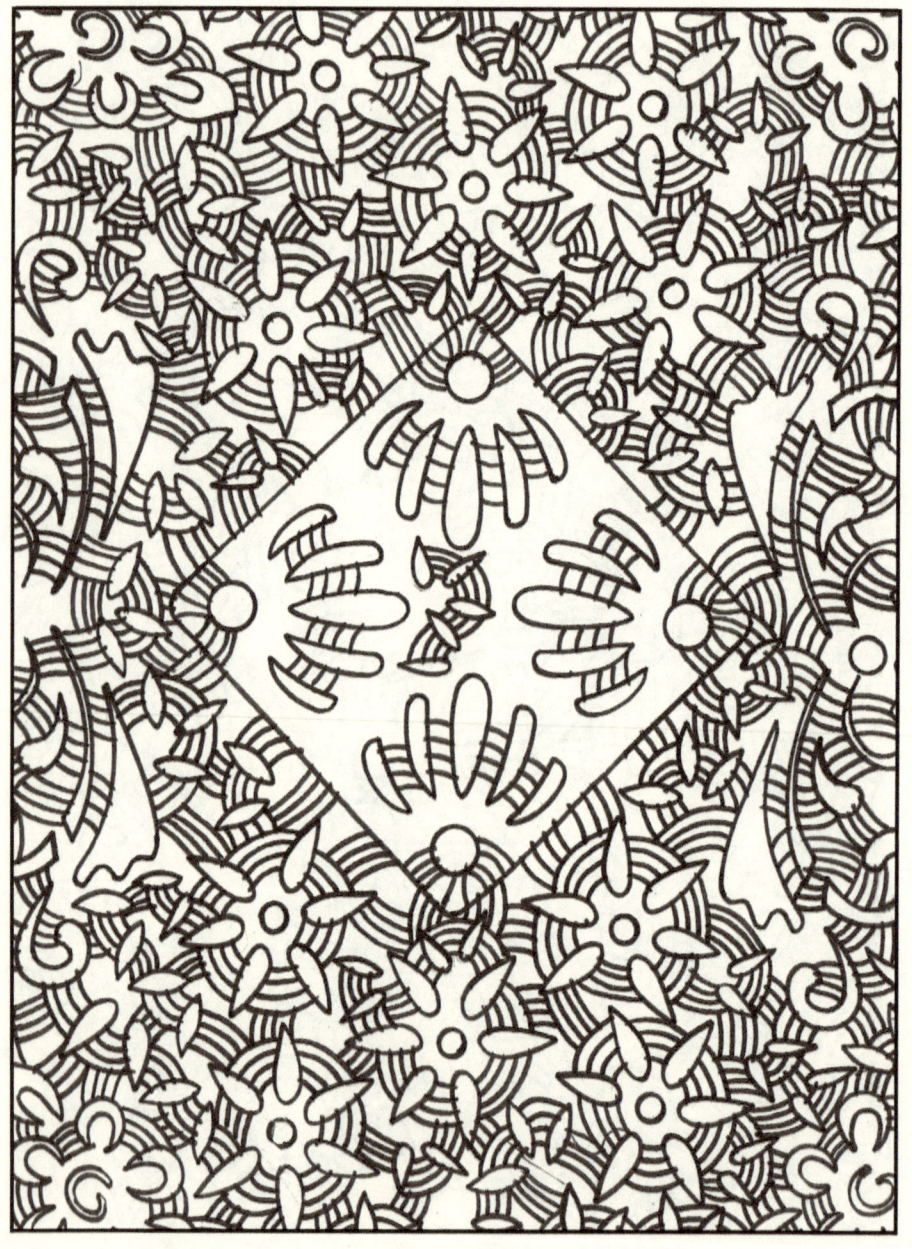

50

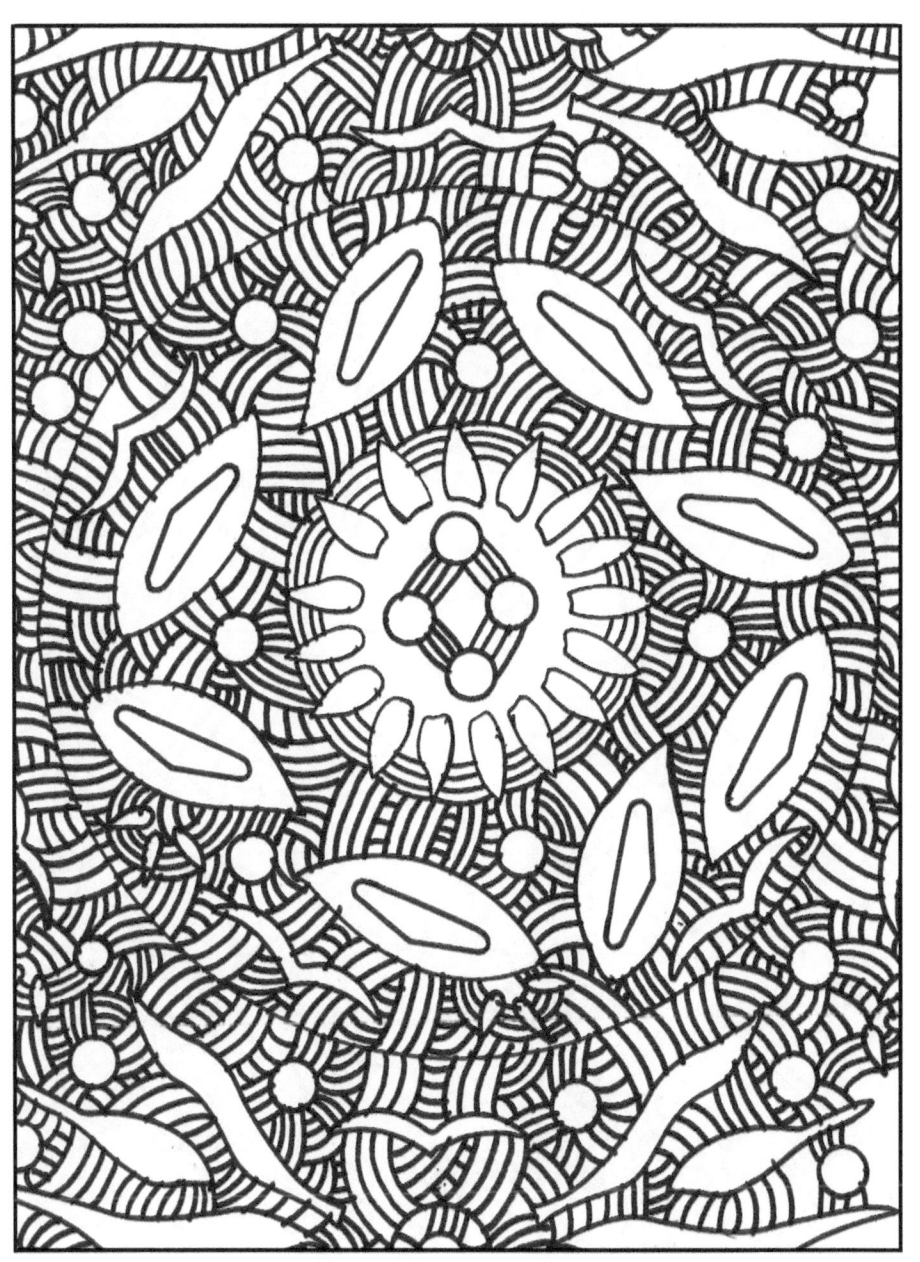

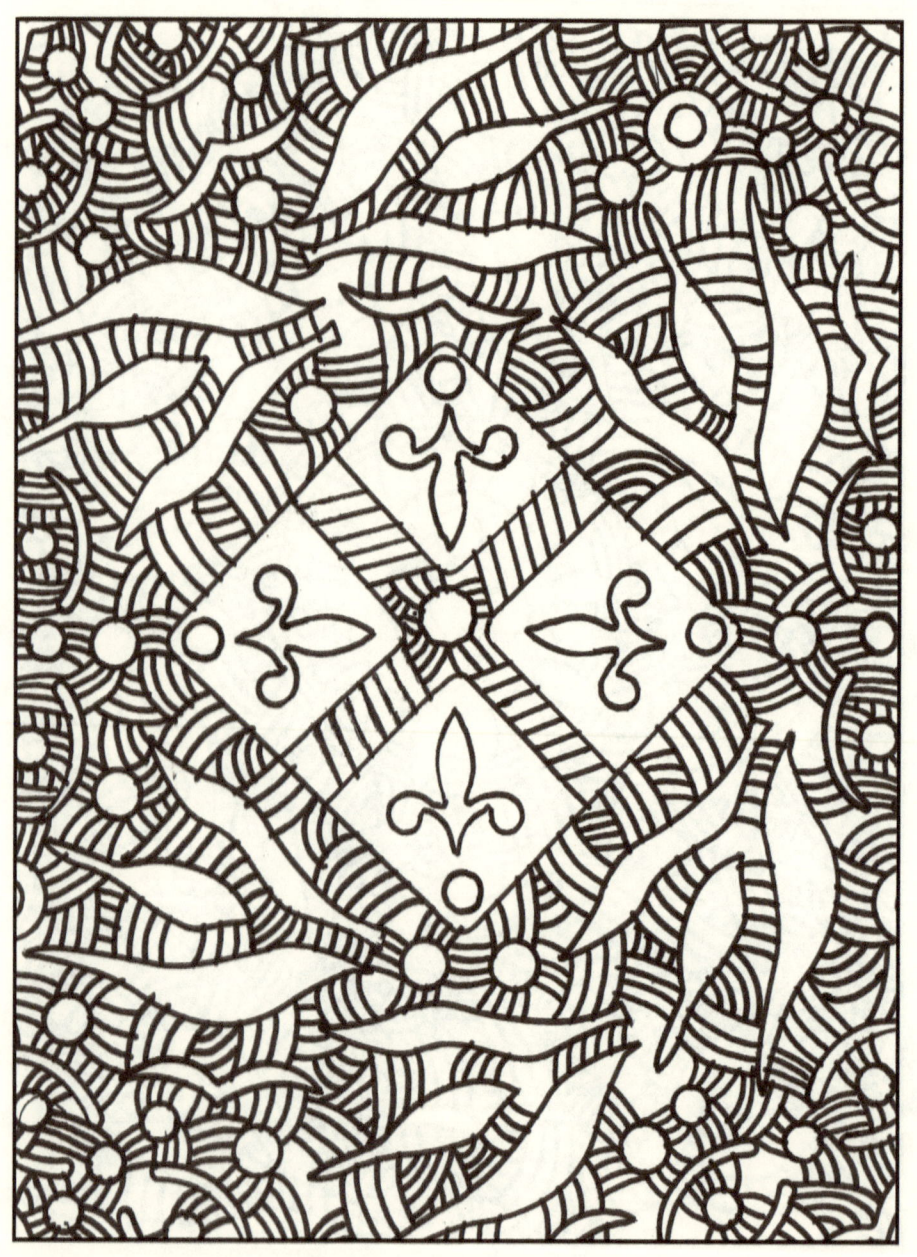

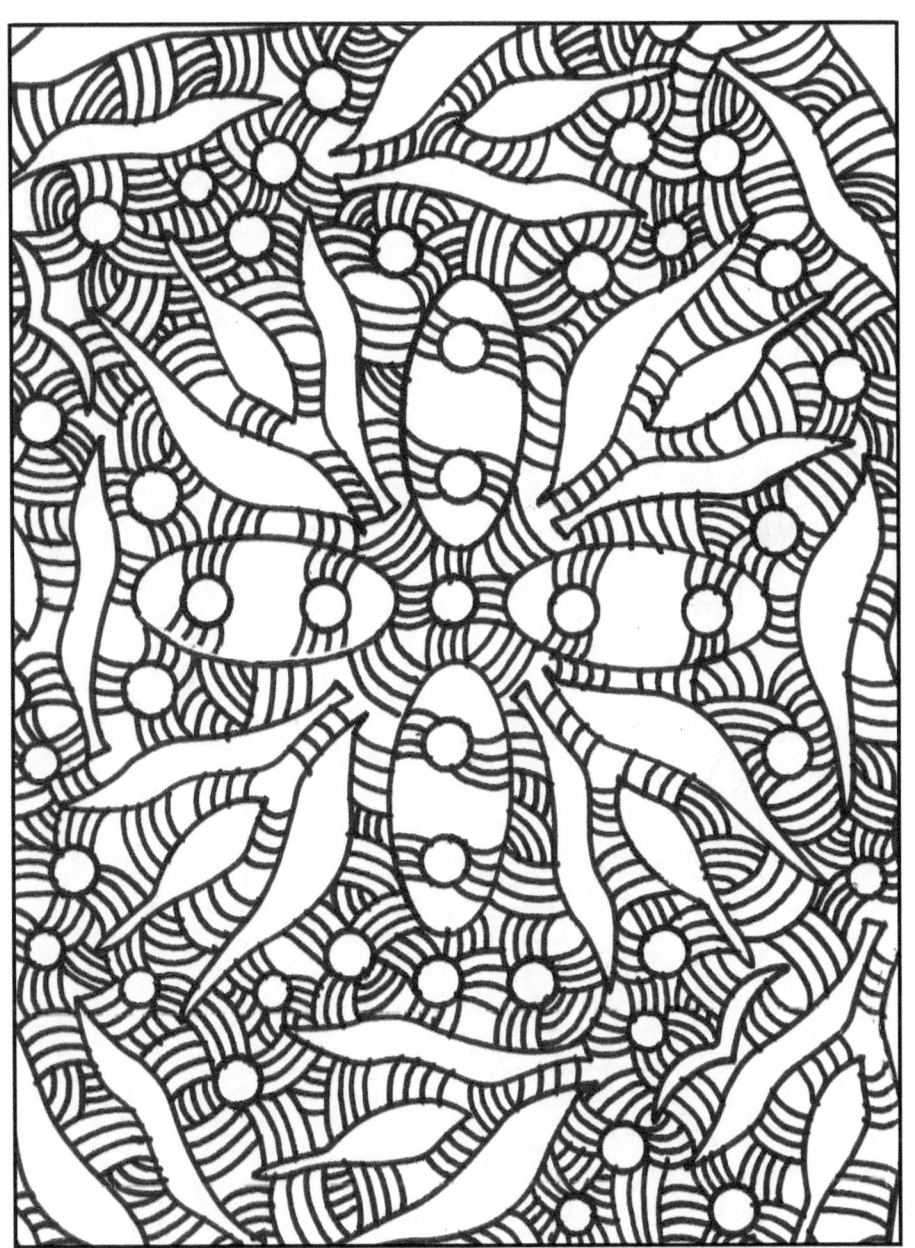

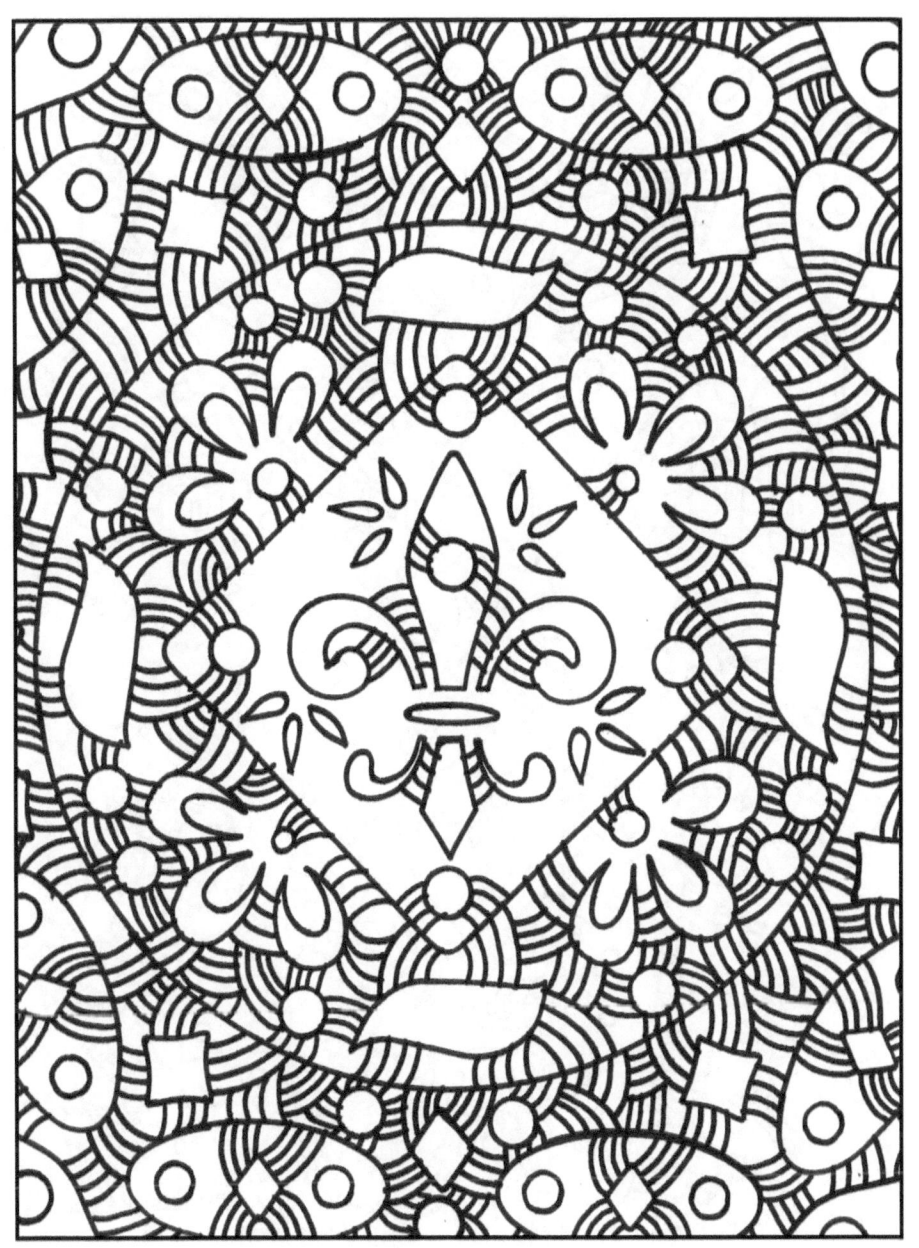

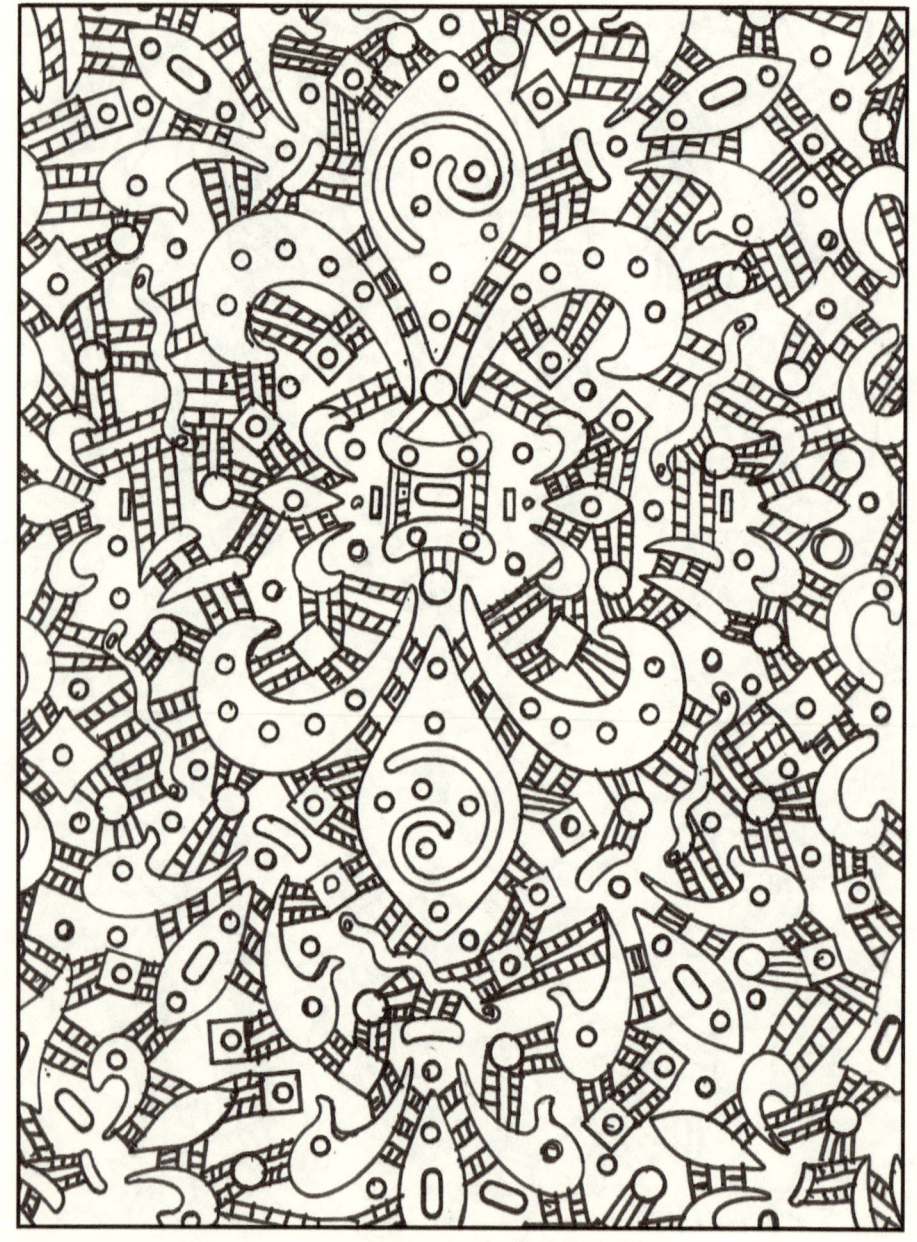

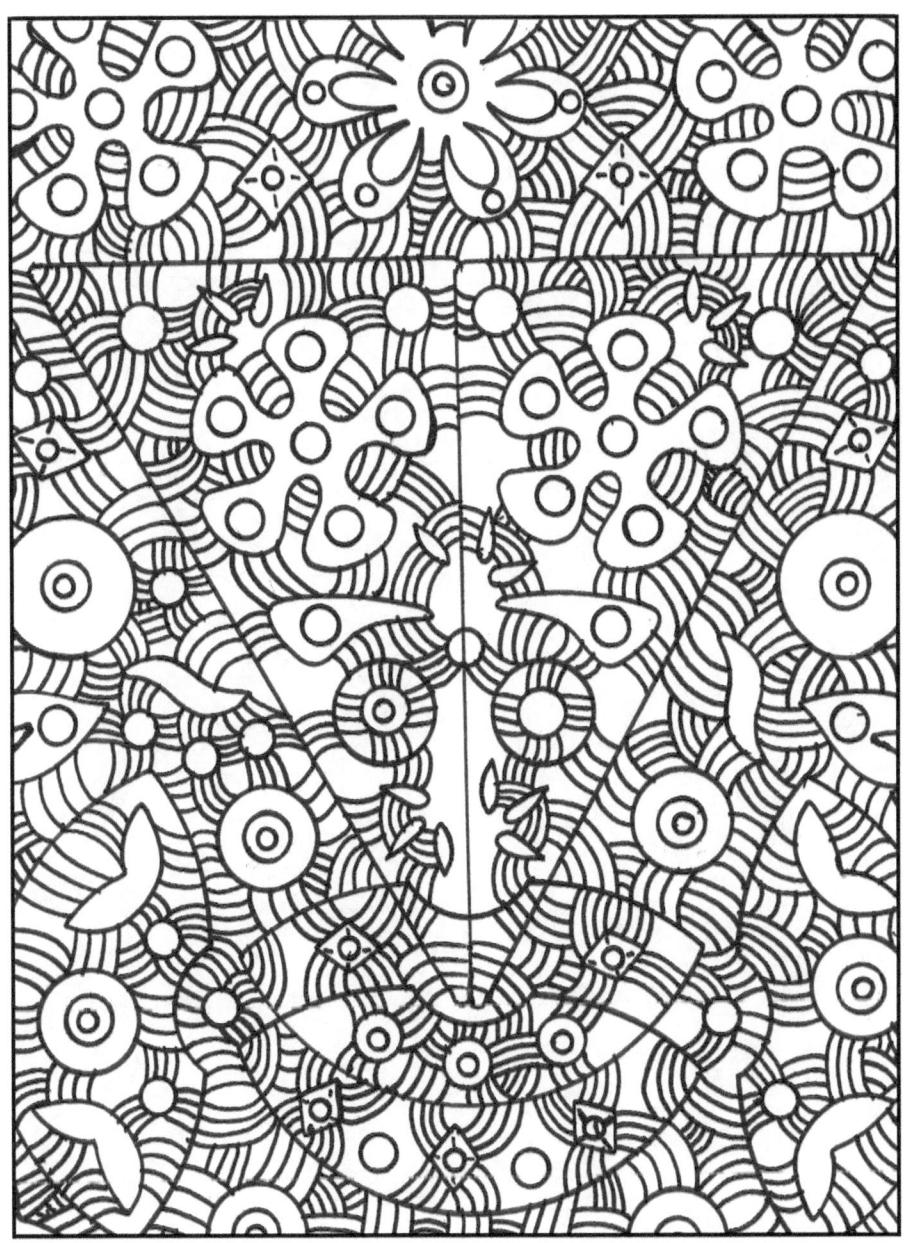

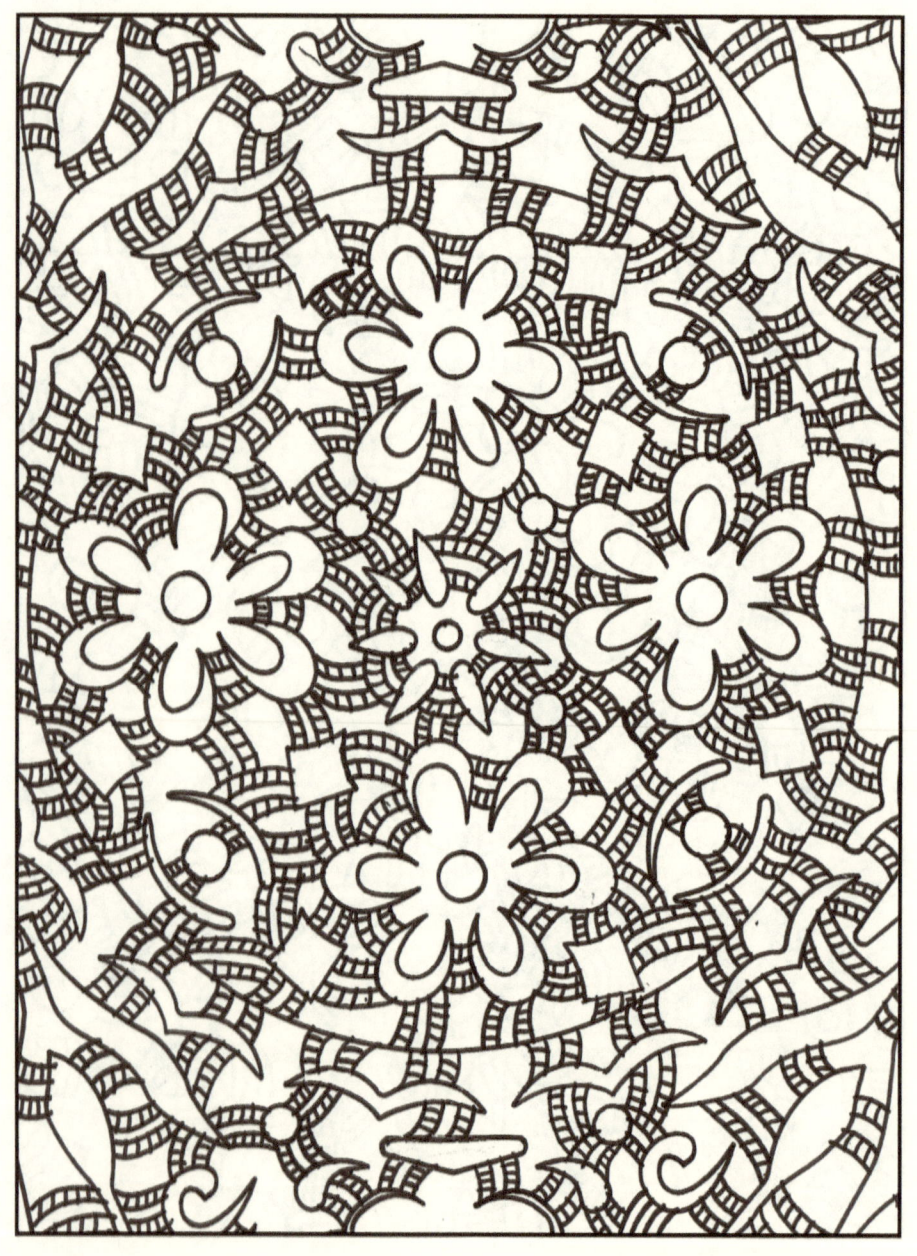

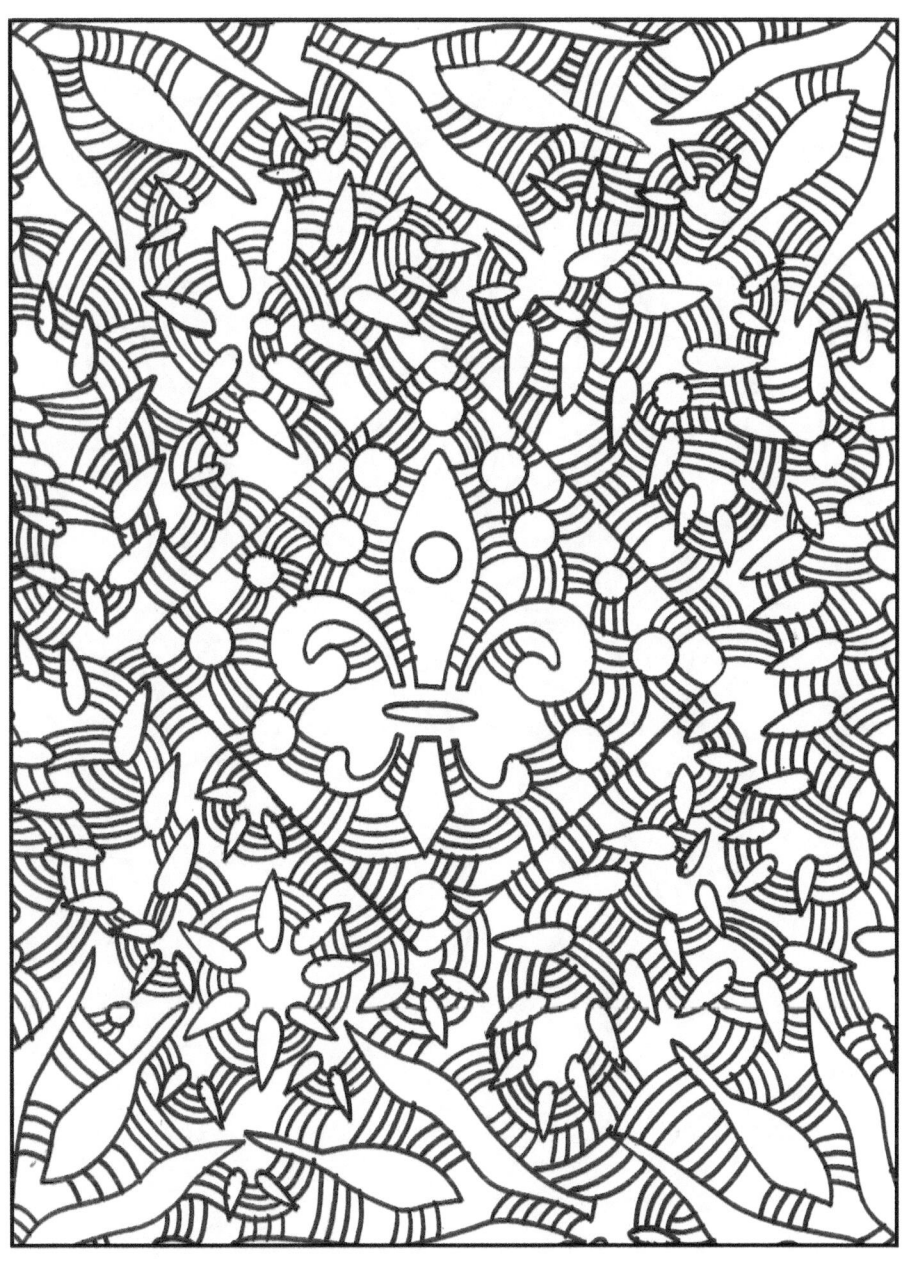

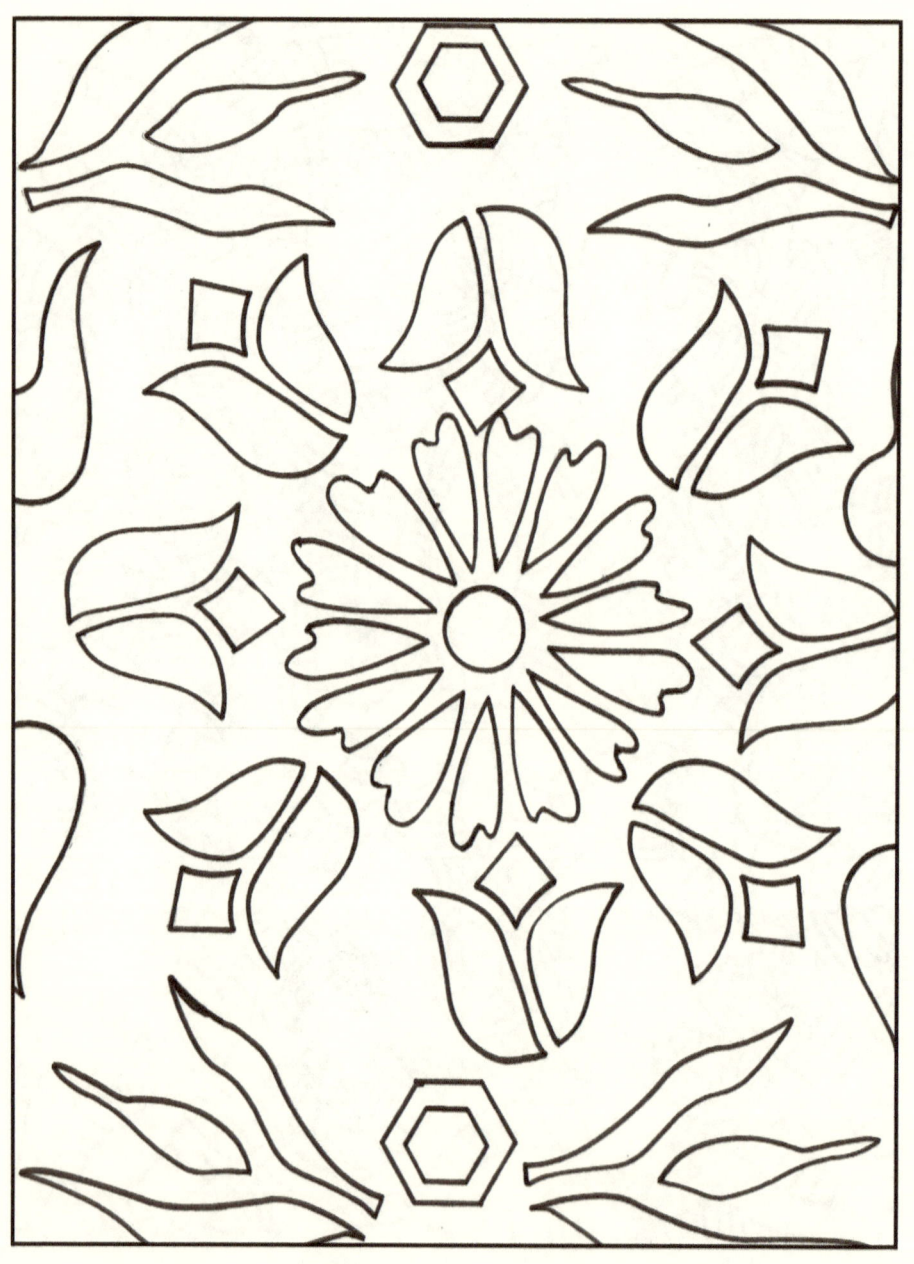

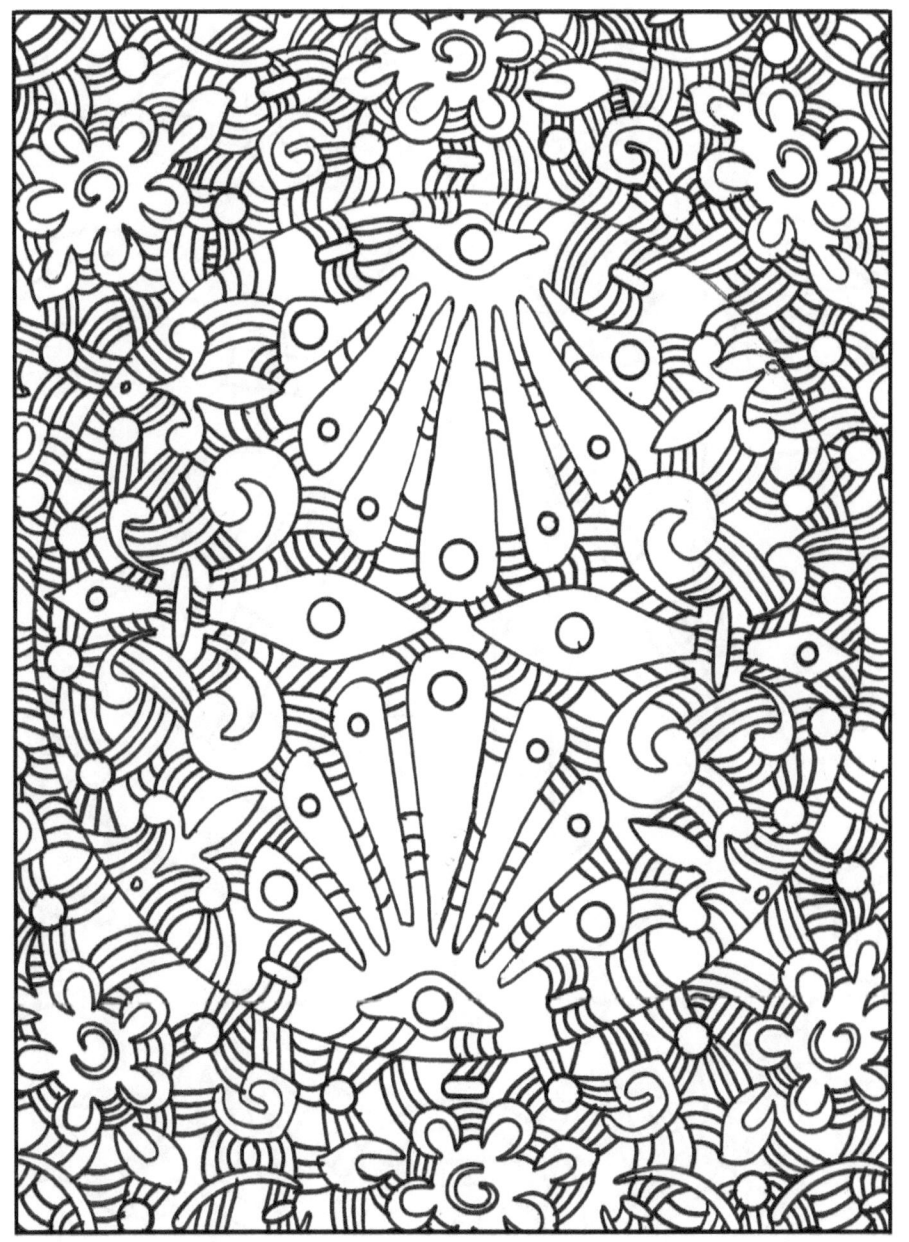

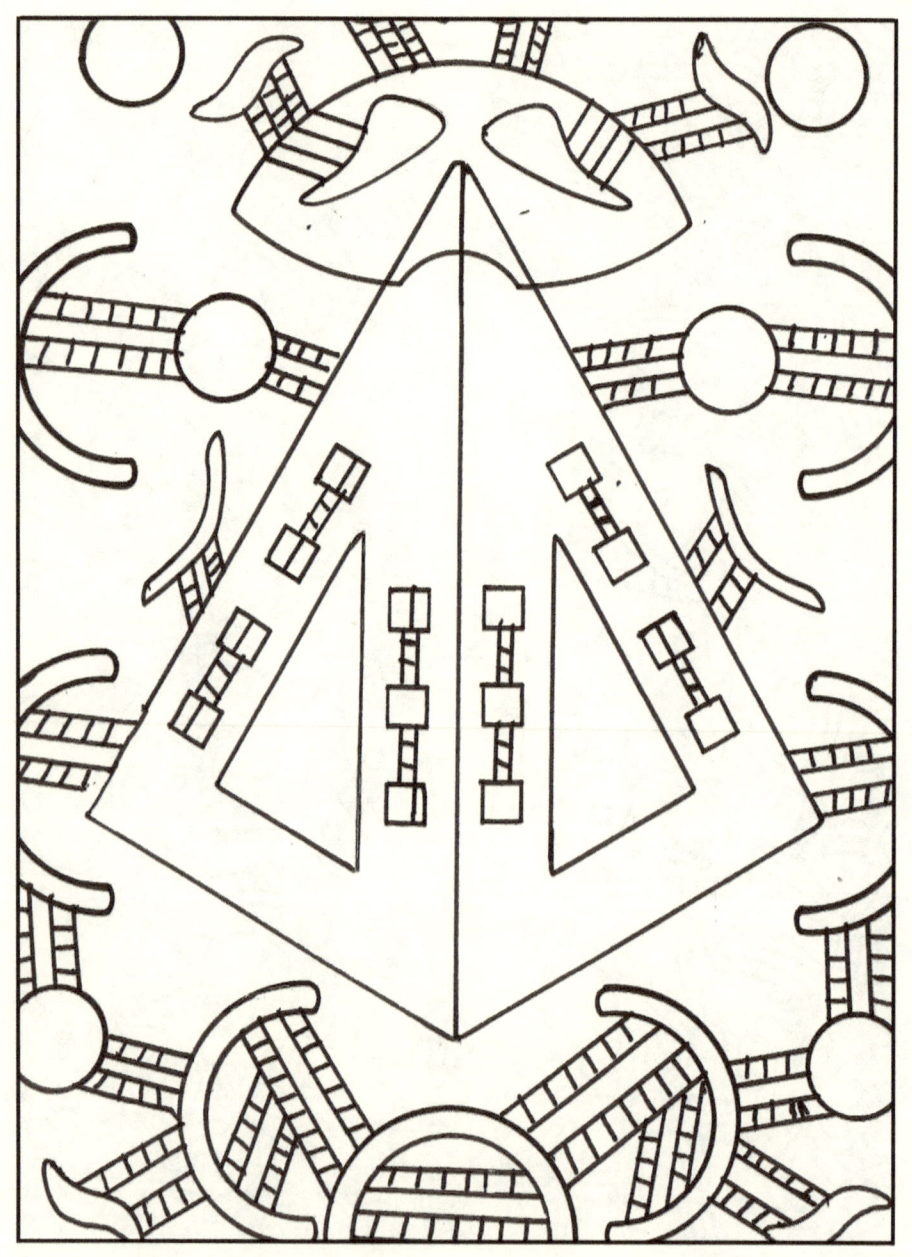

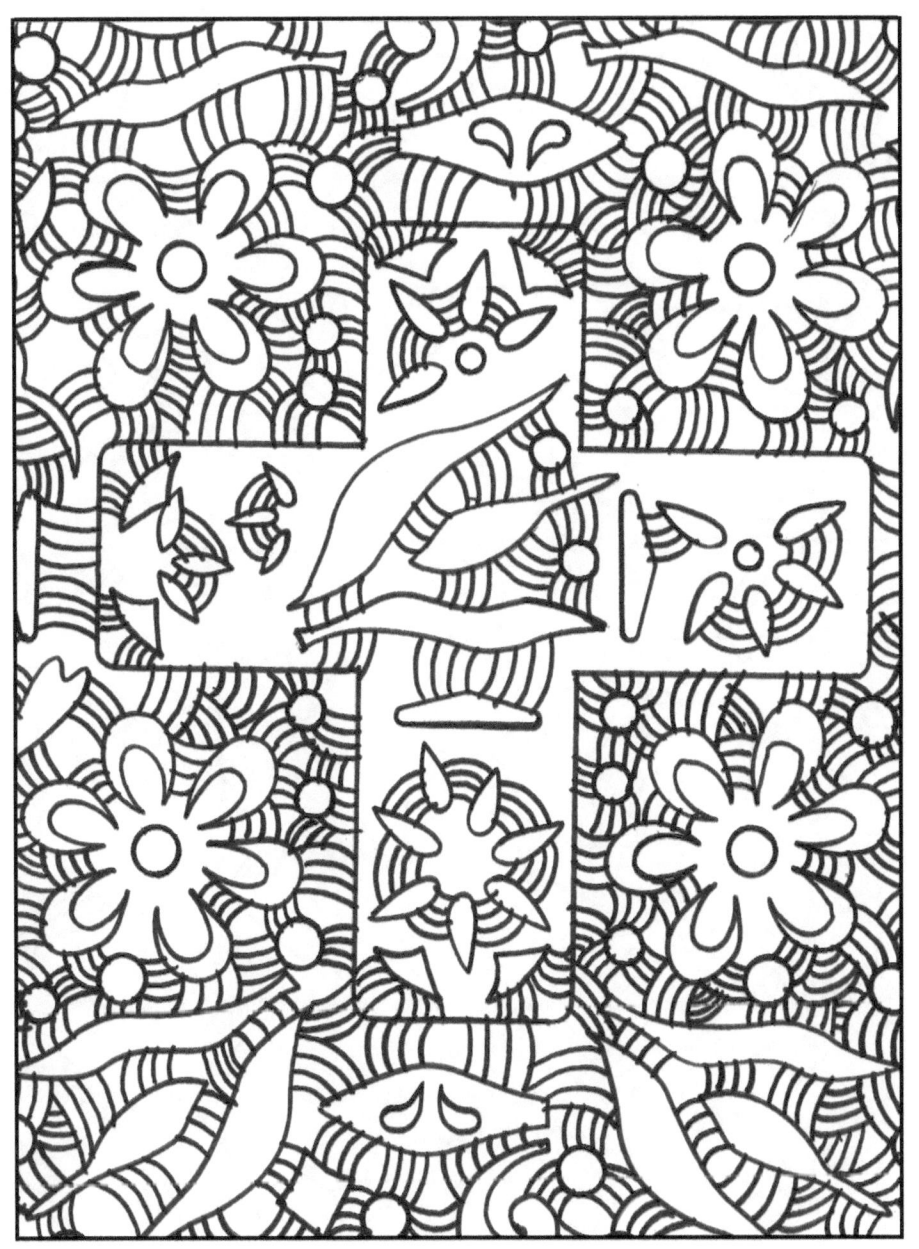

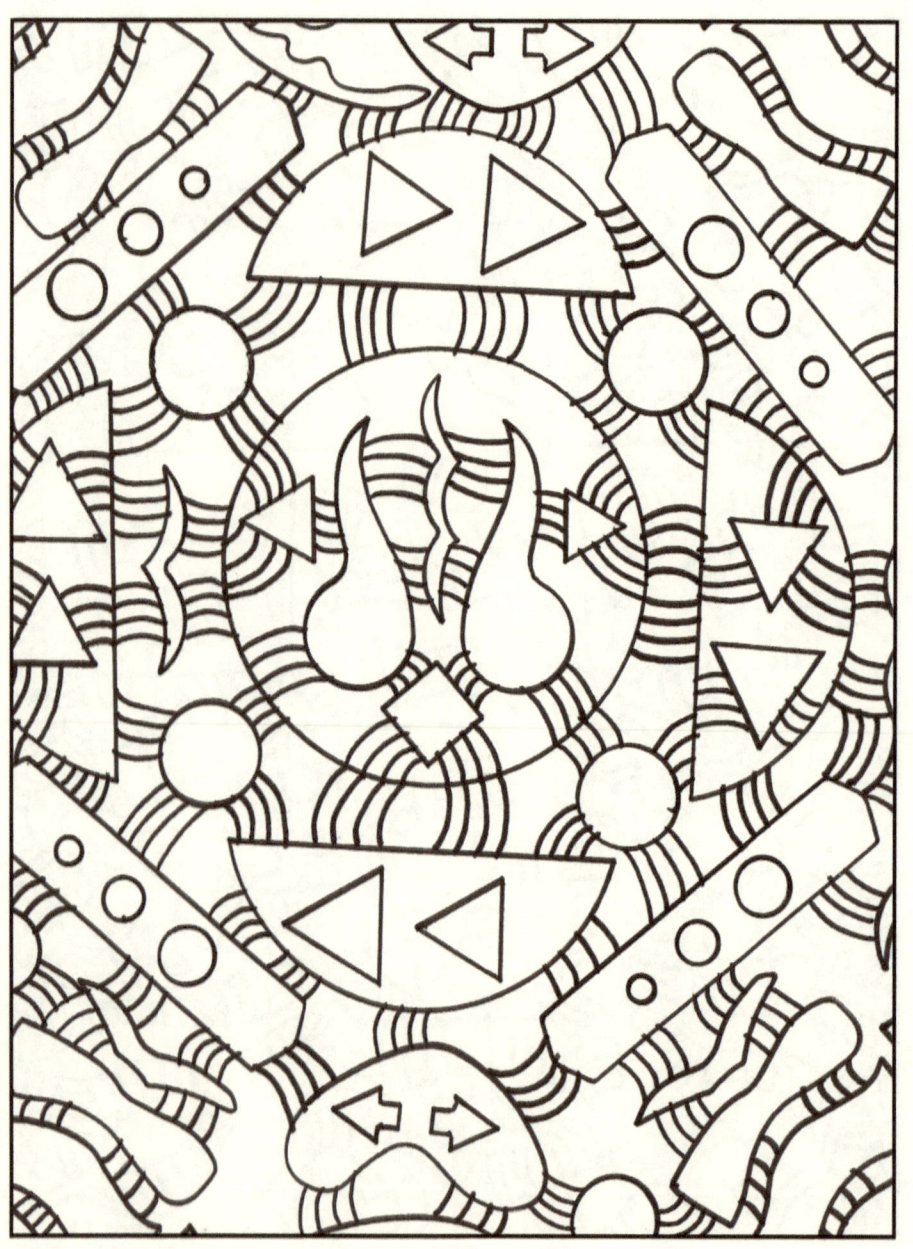

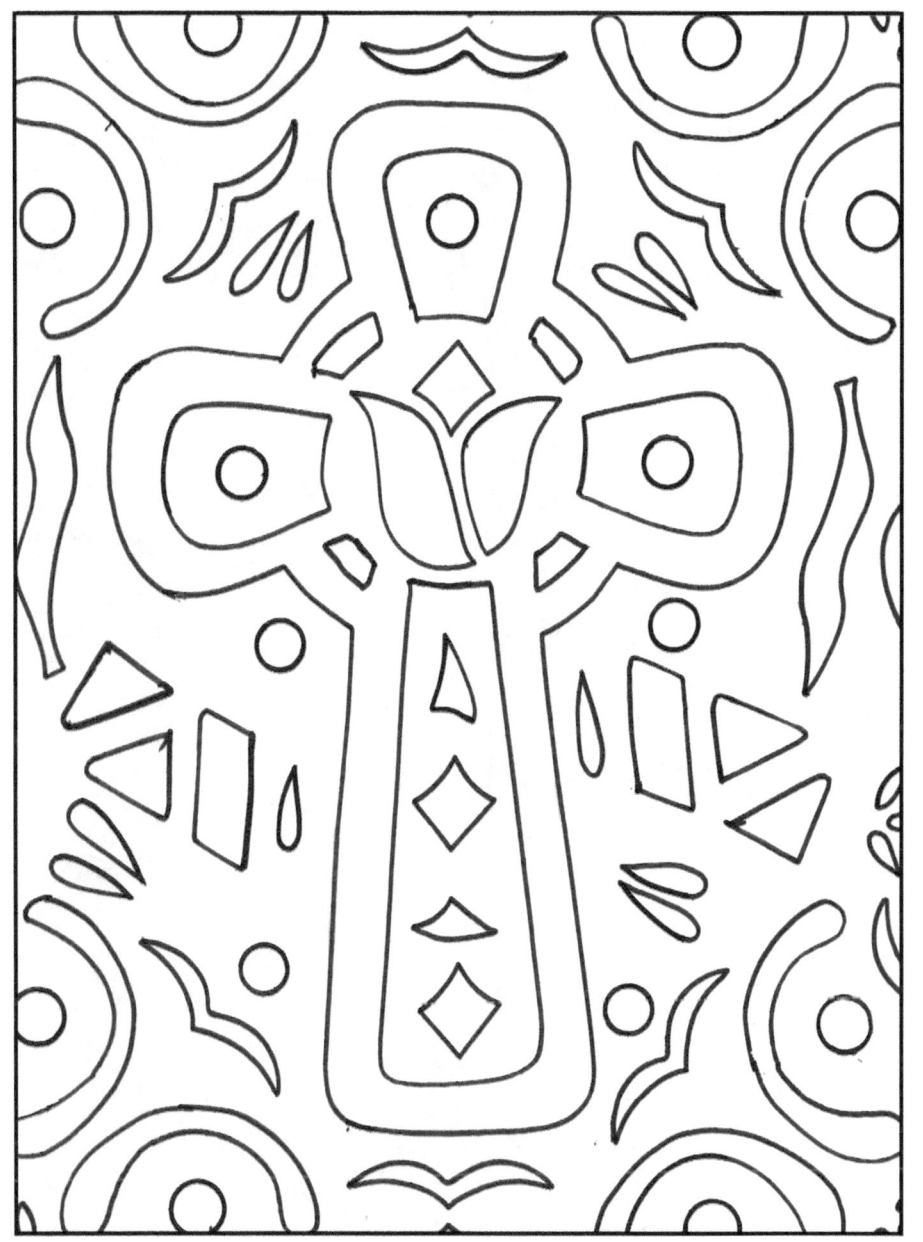

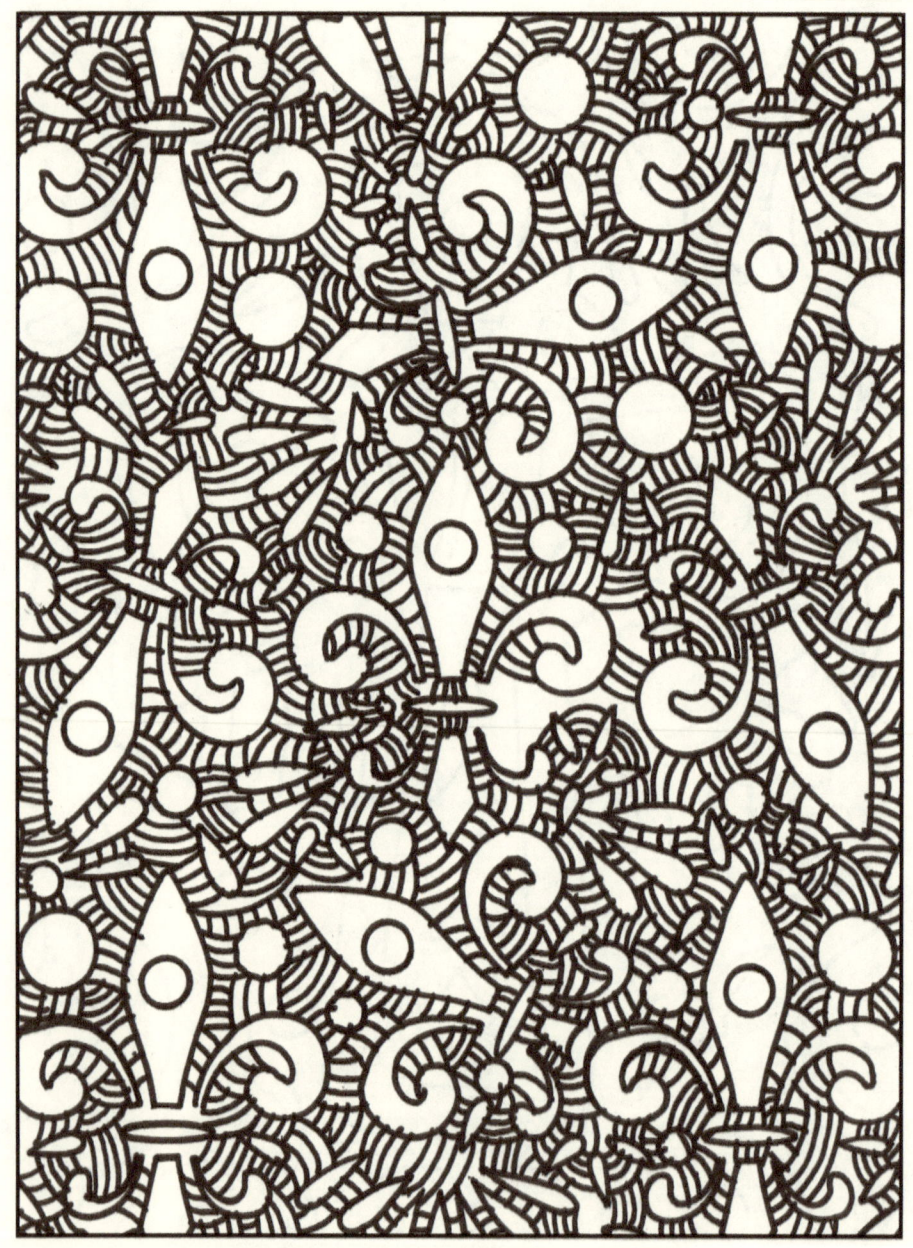

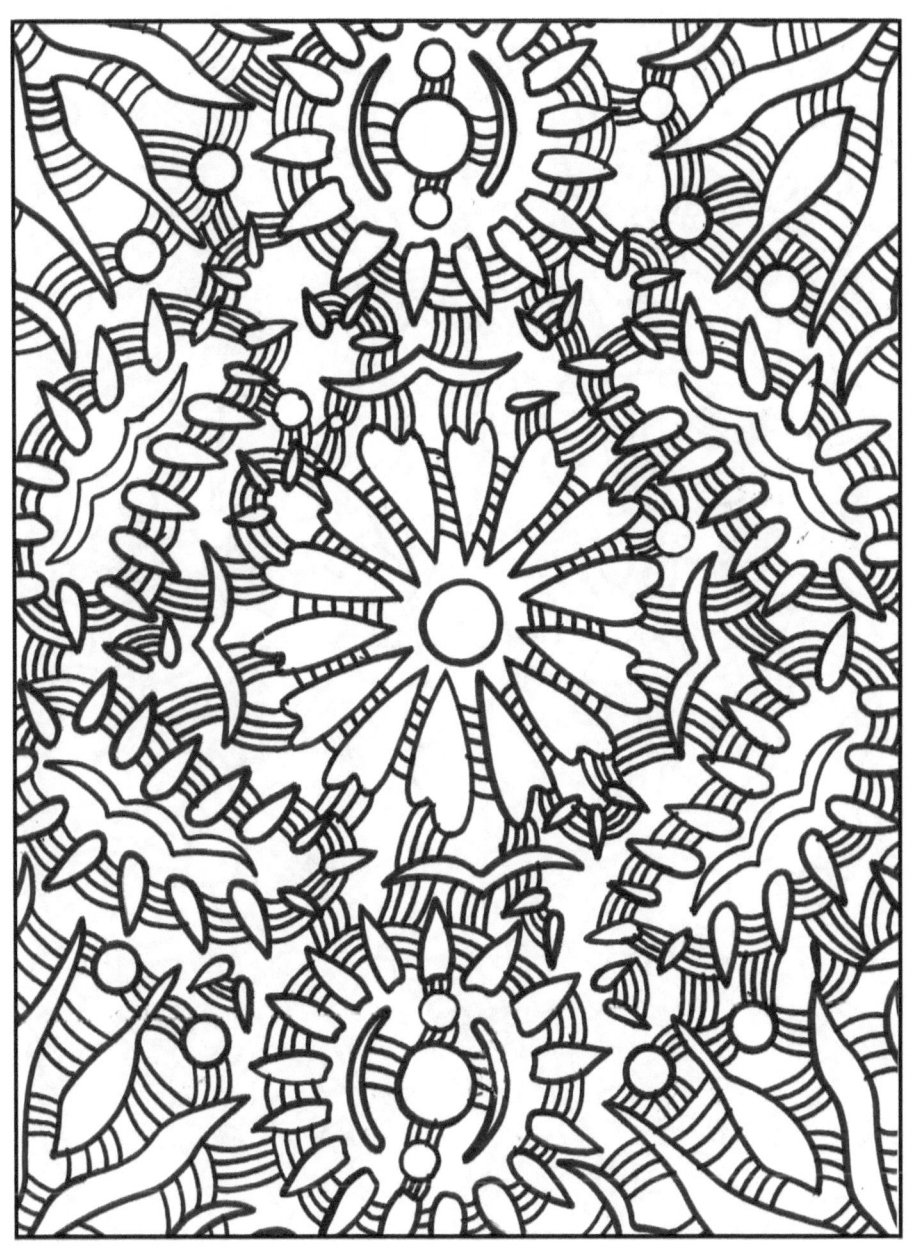

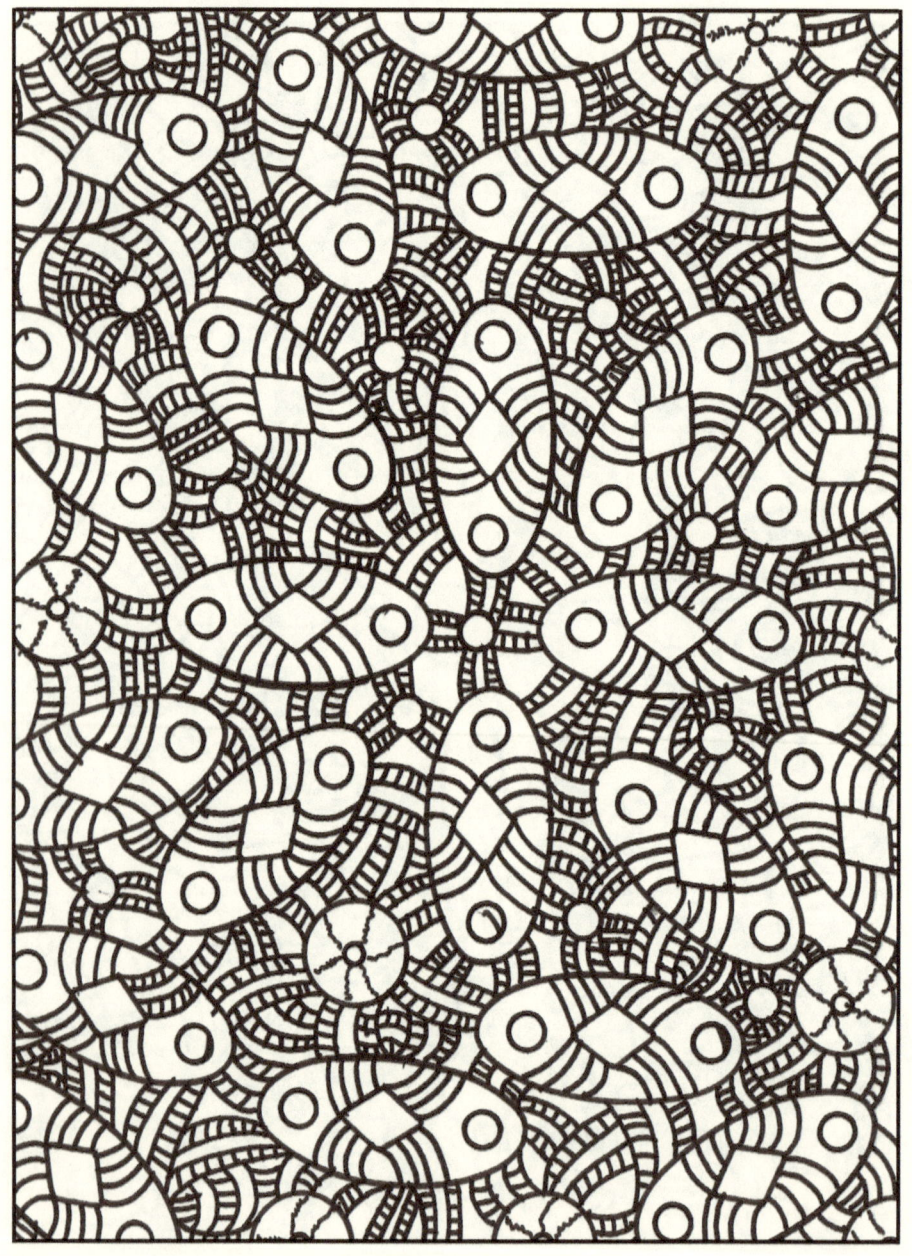

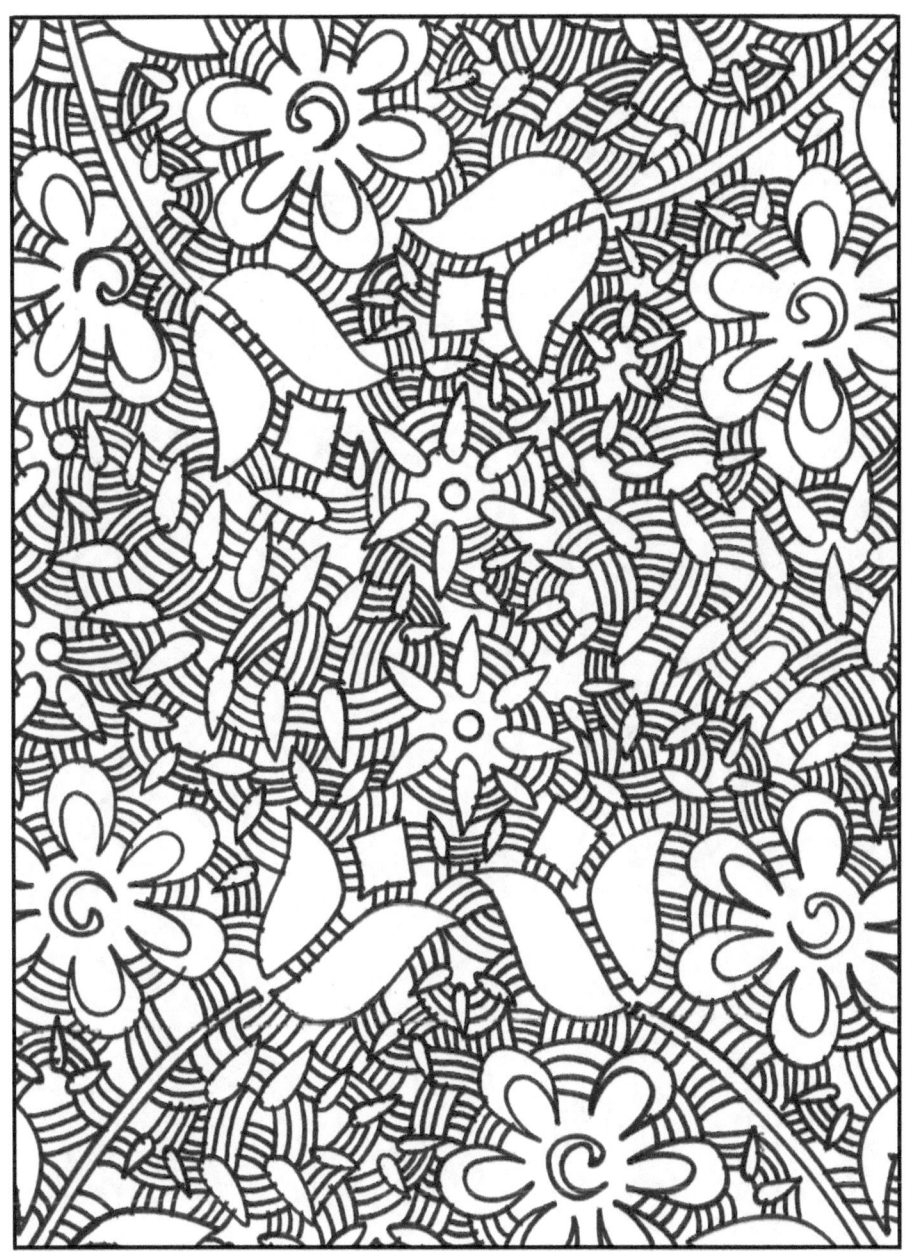

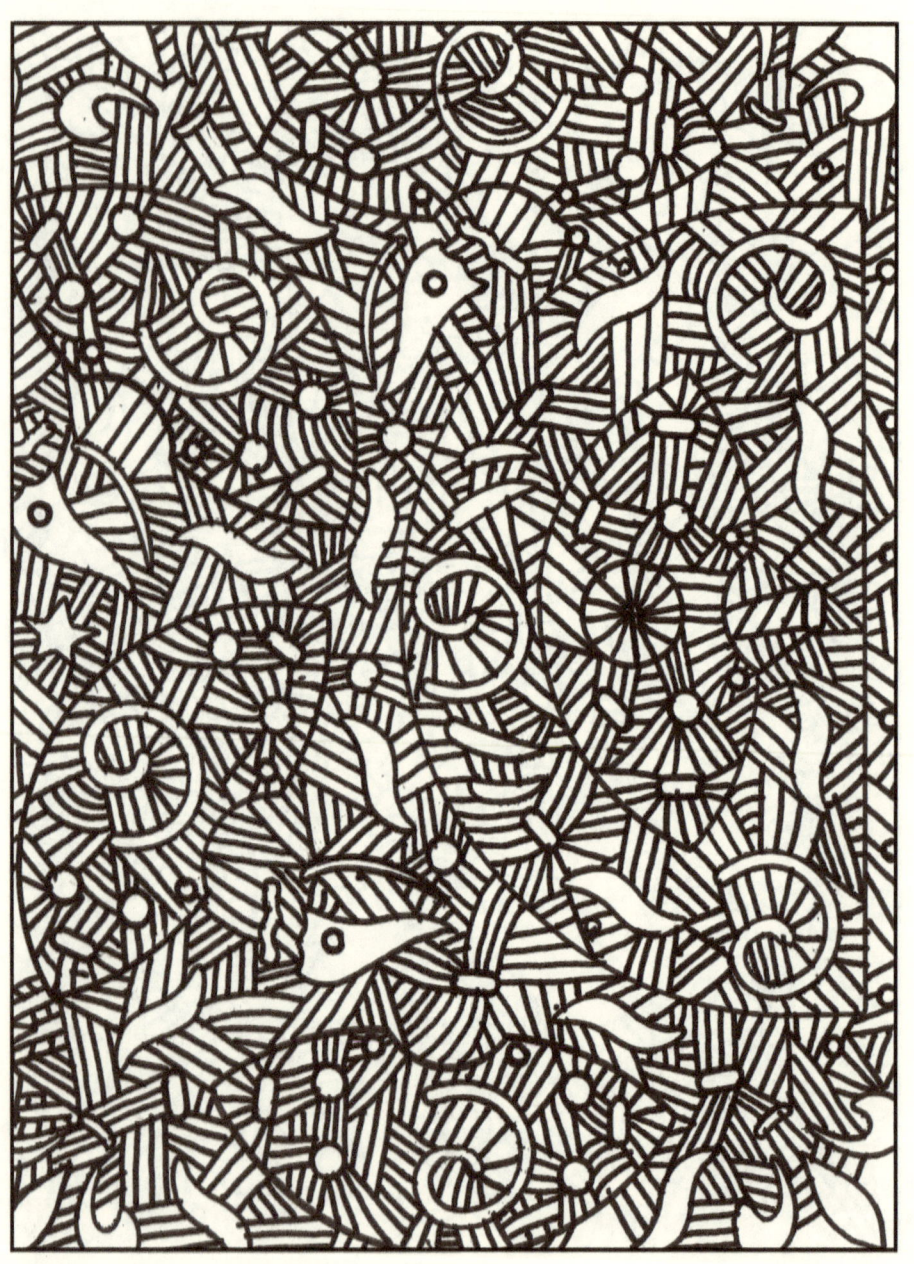

70

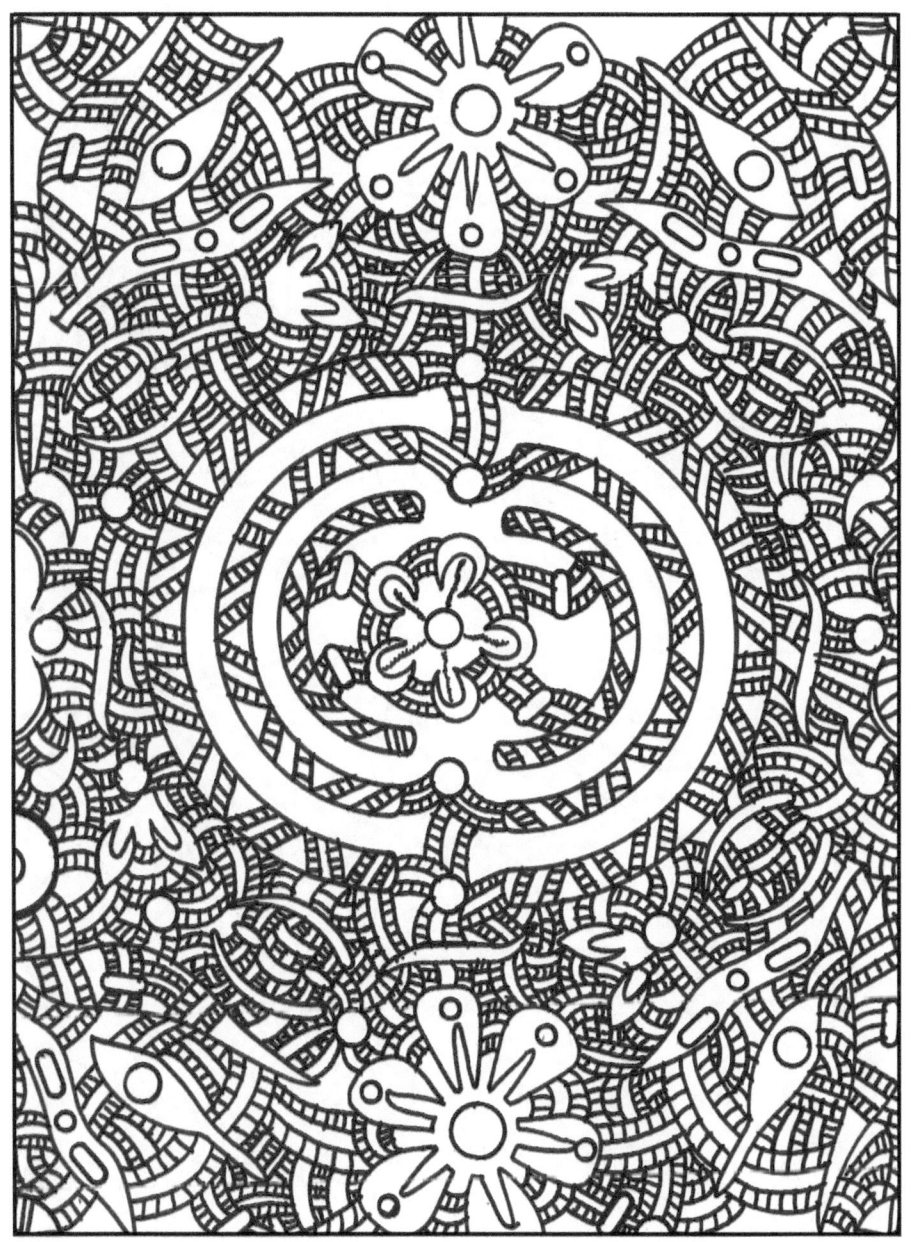

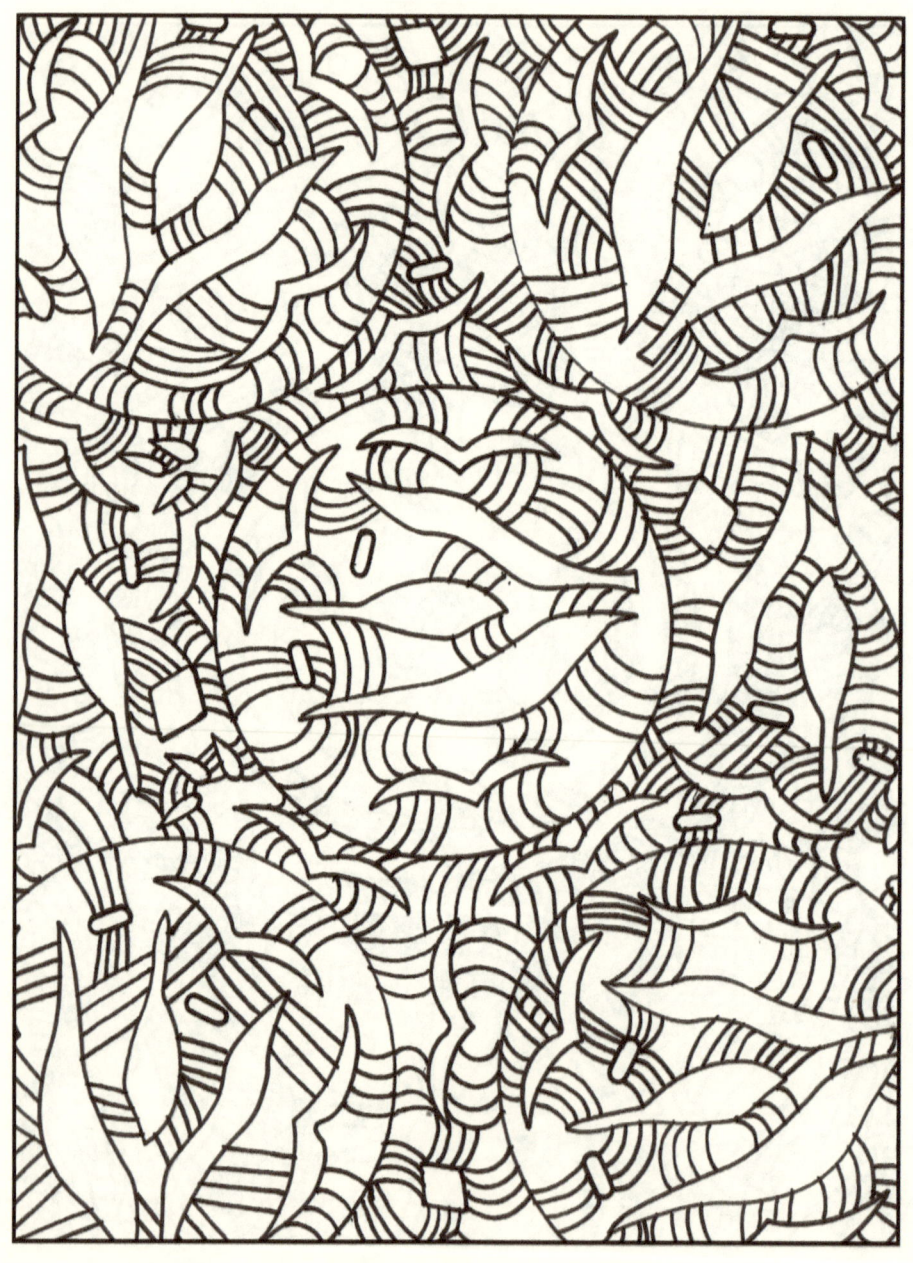

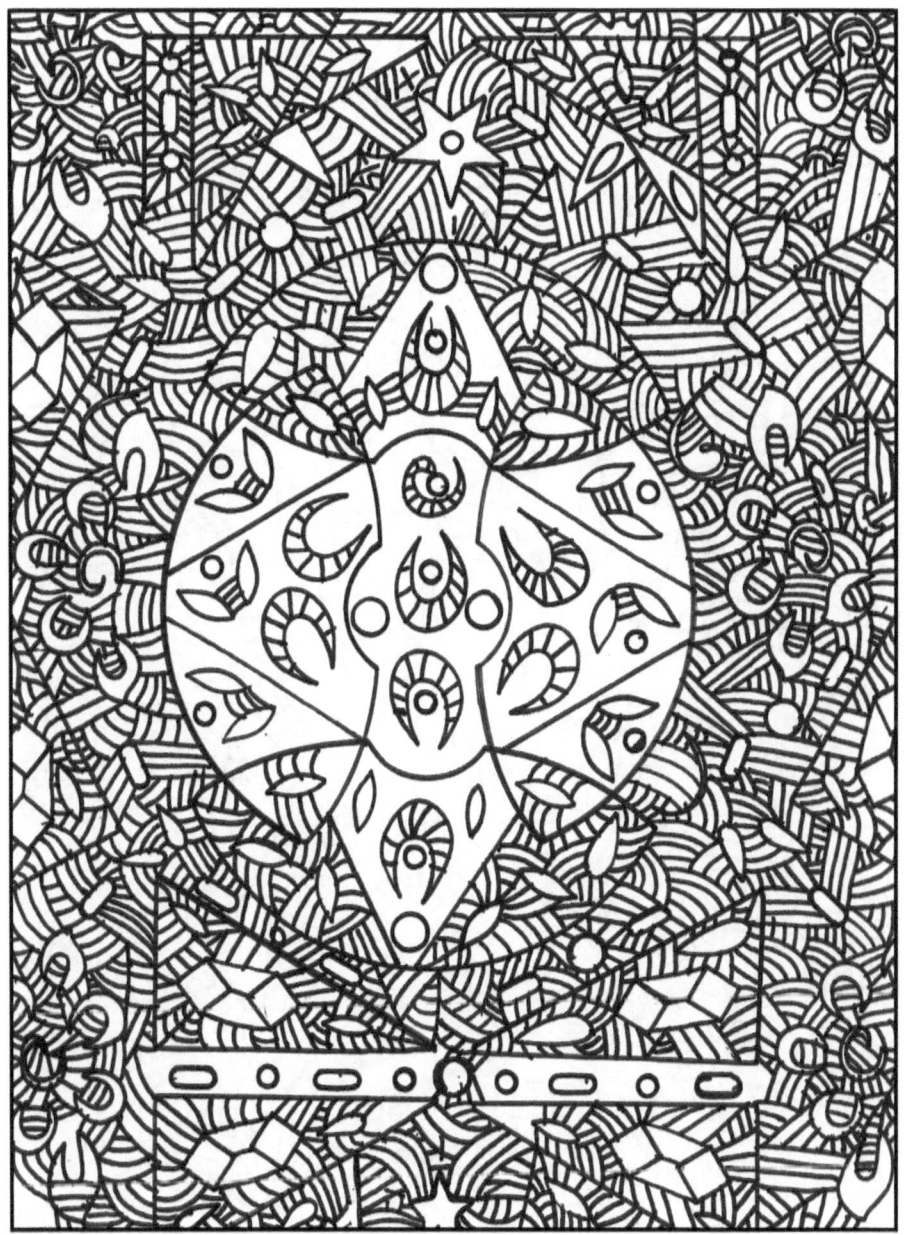

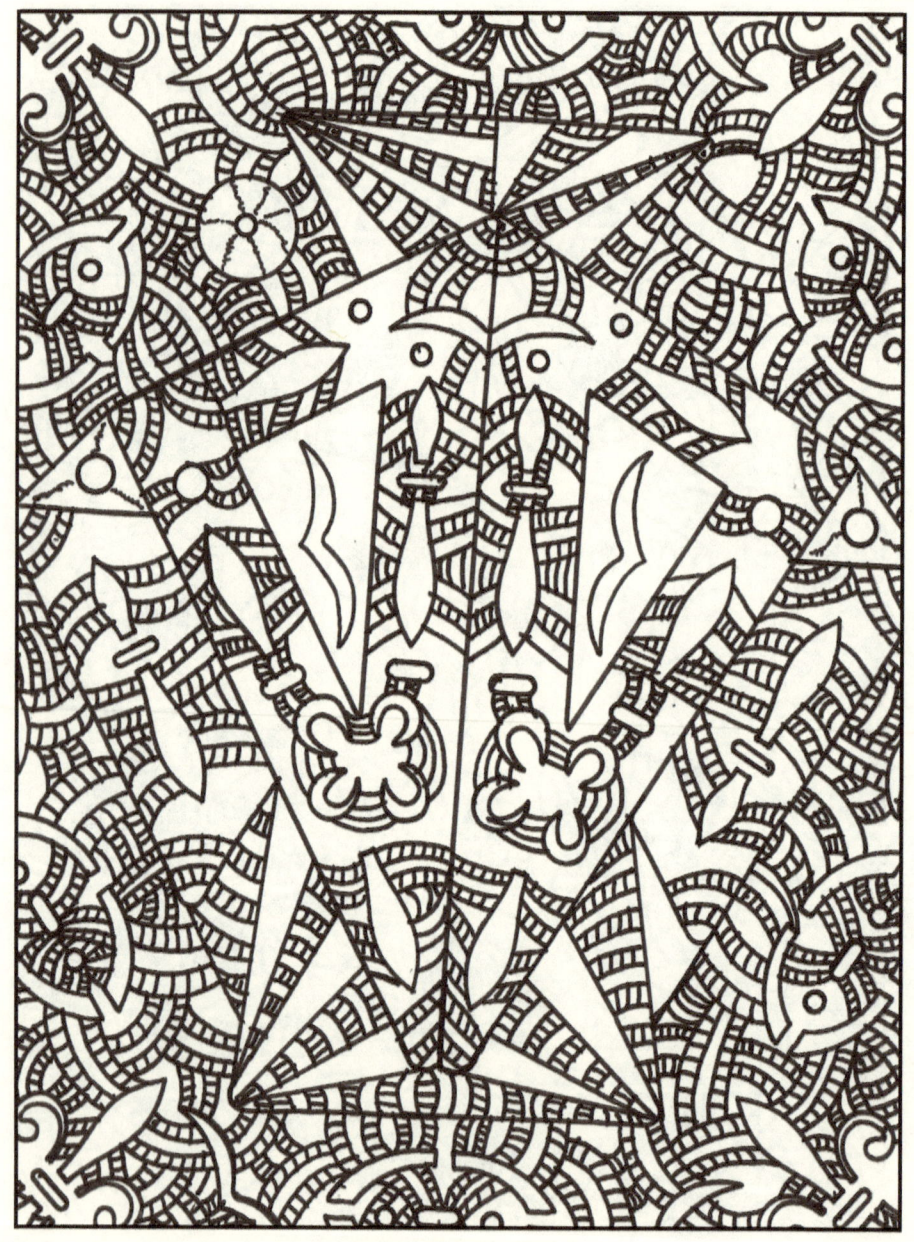

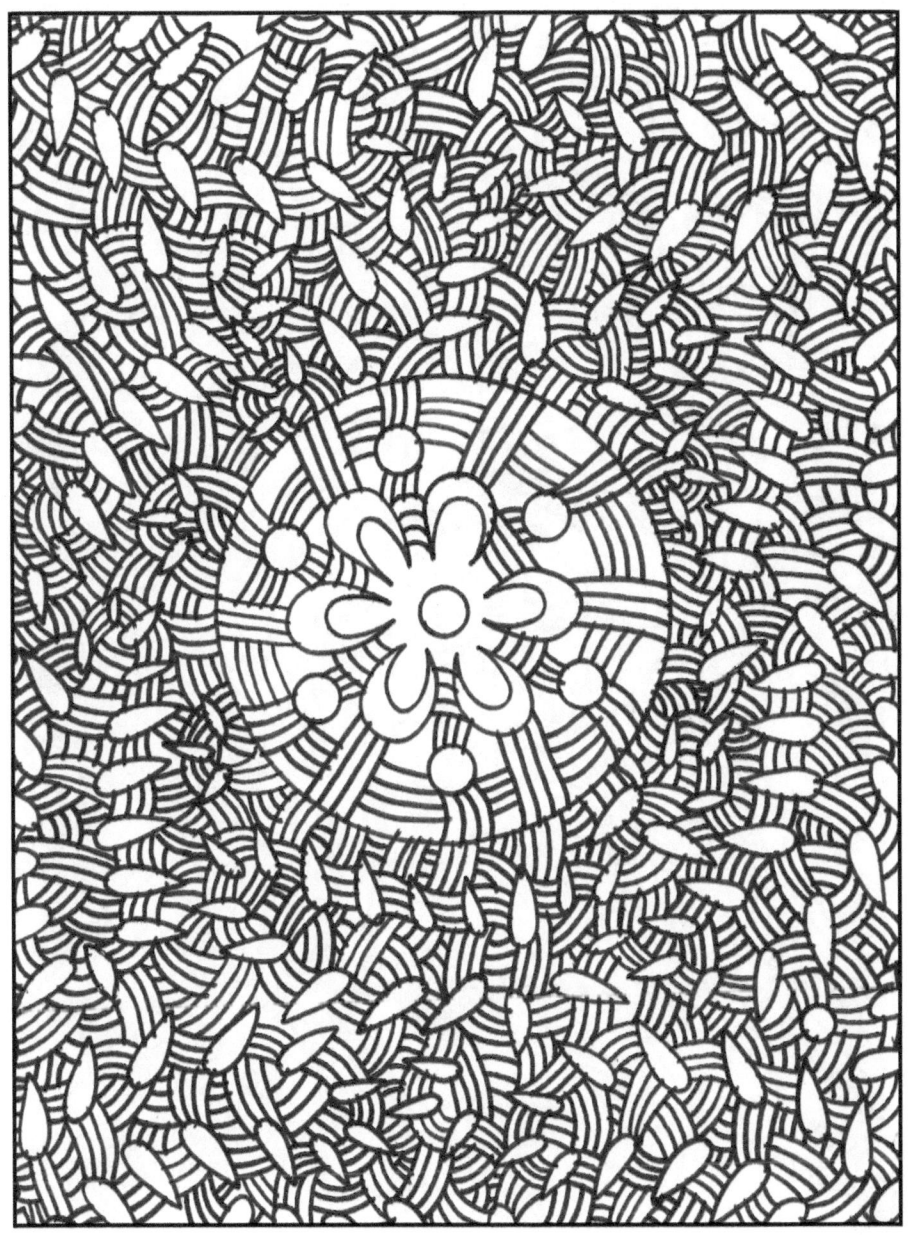

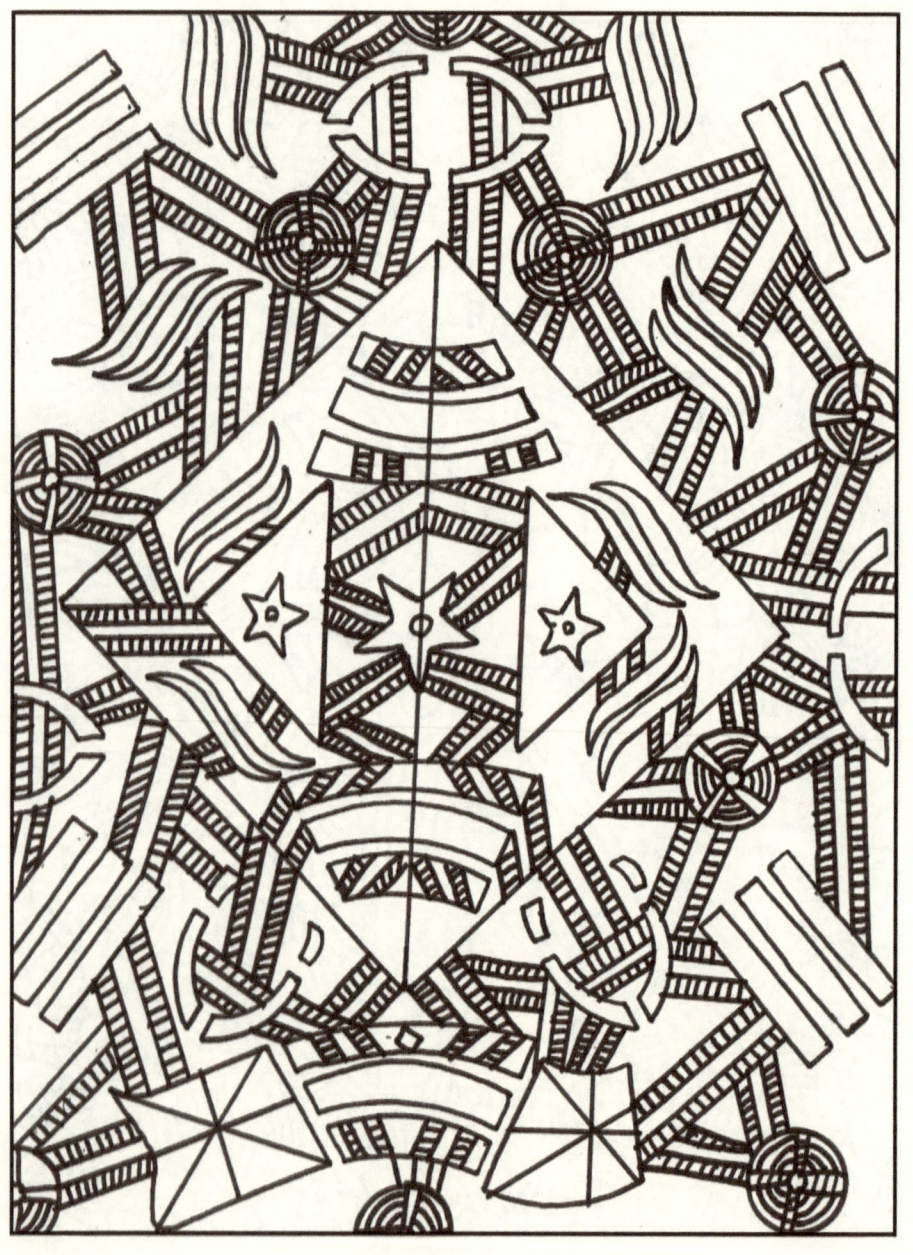

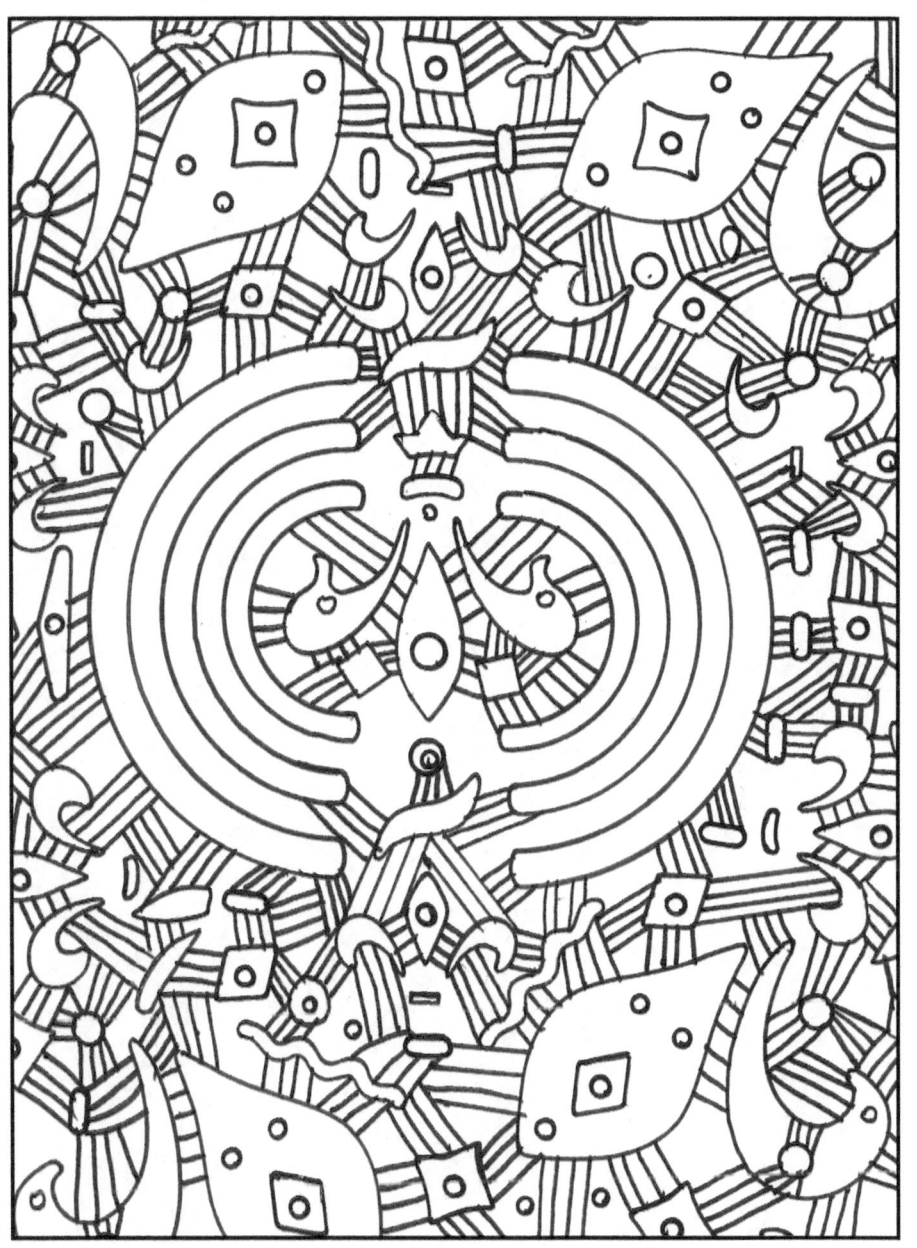

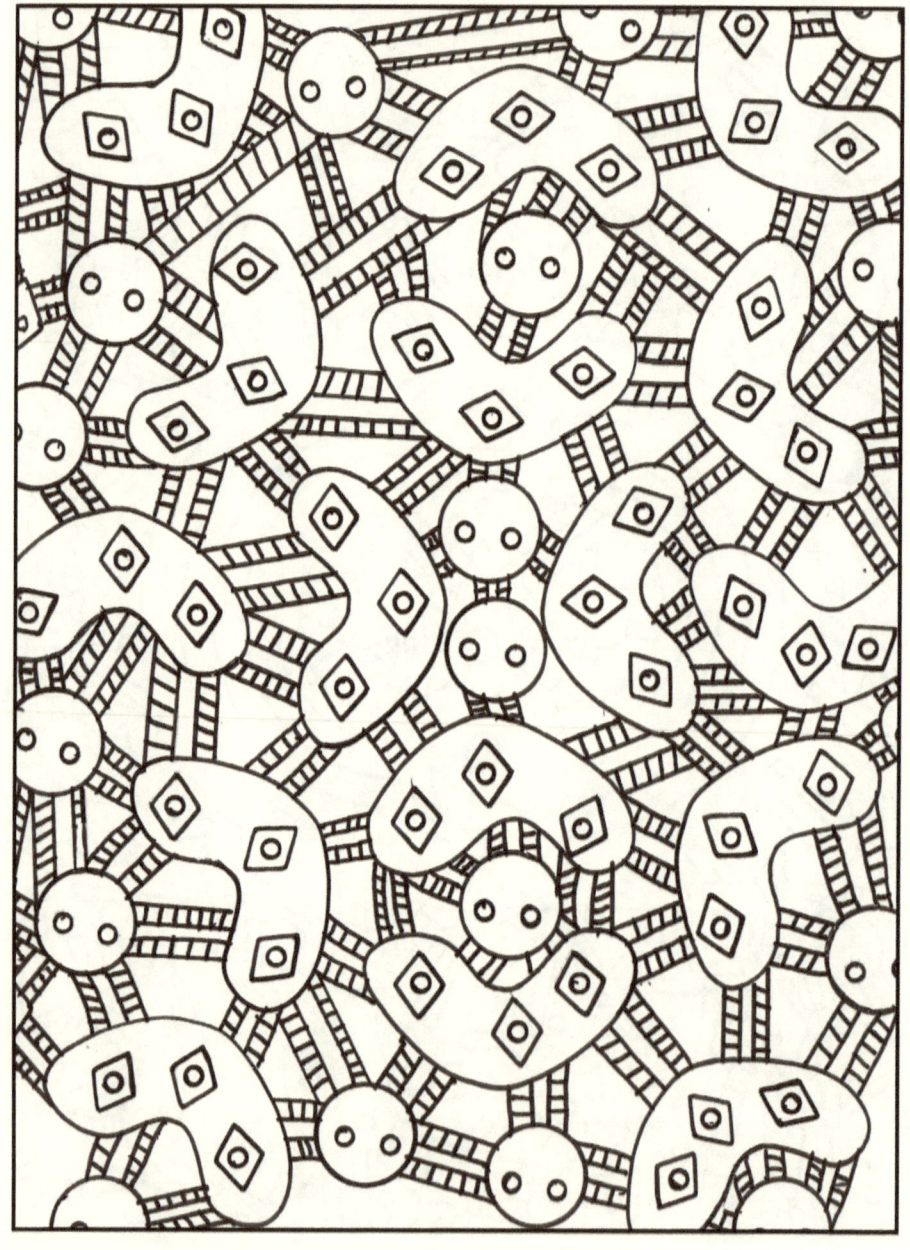

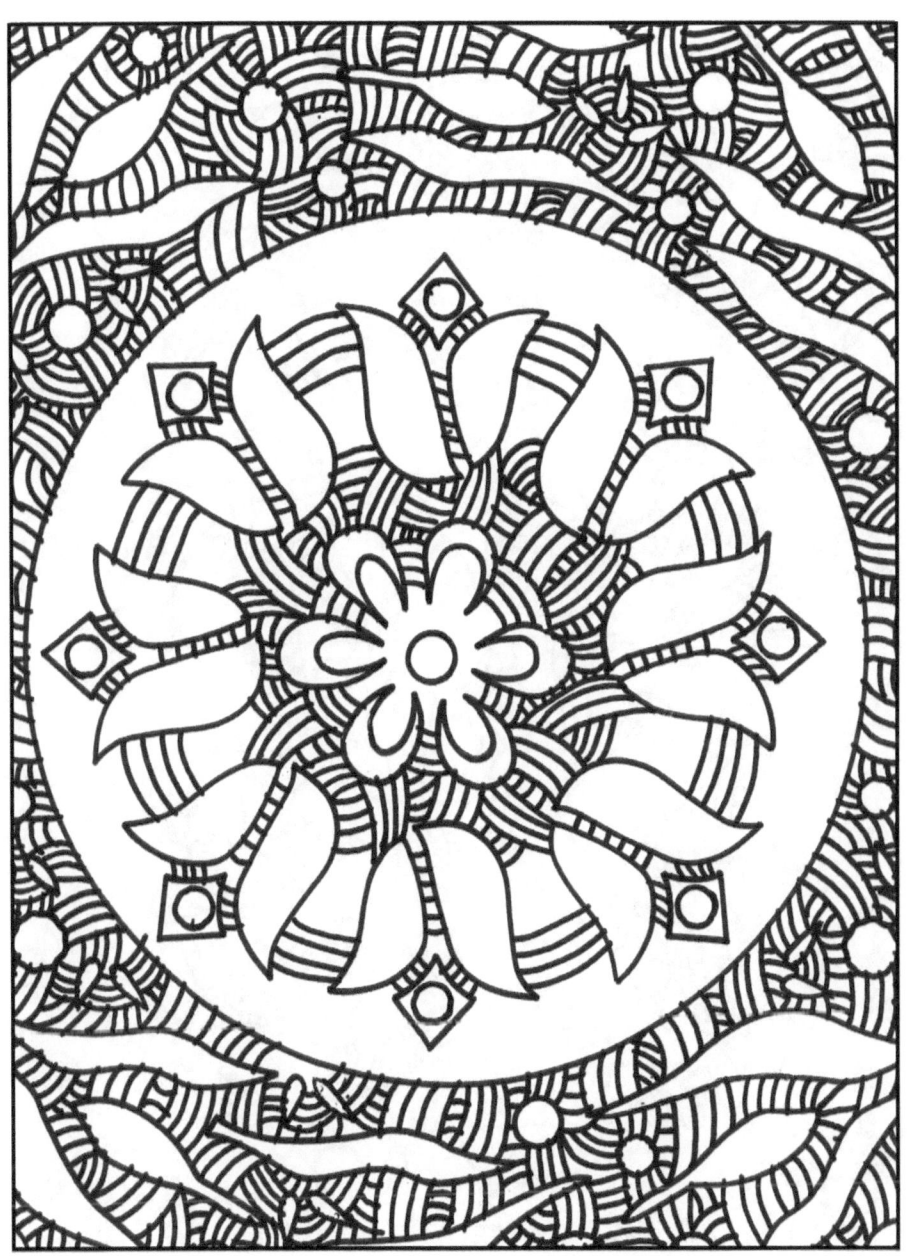

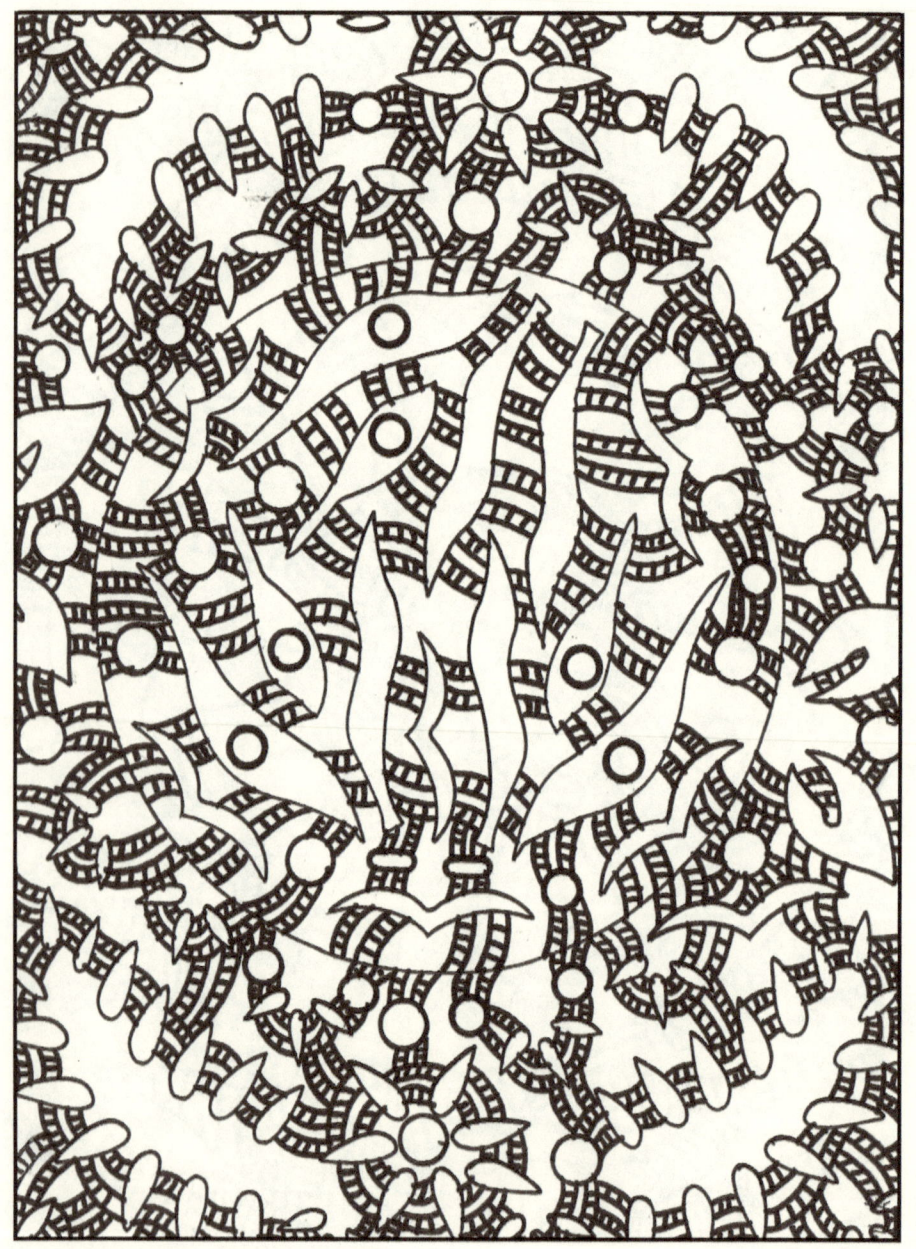

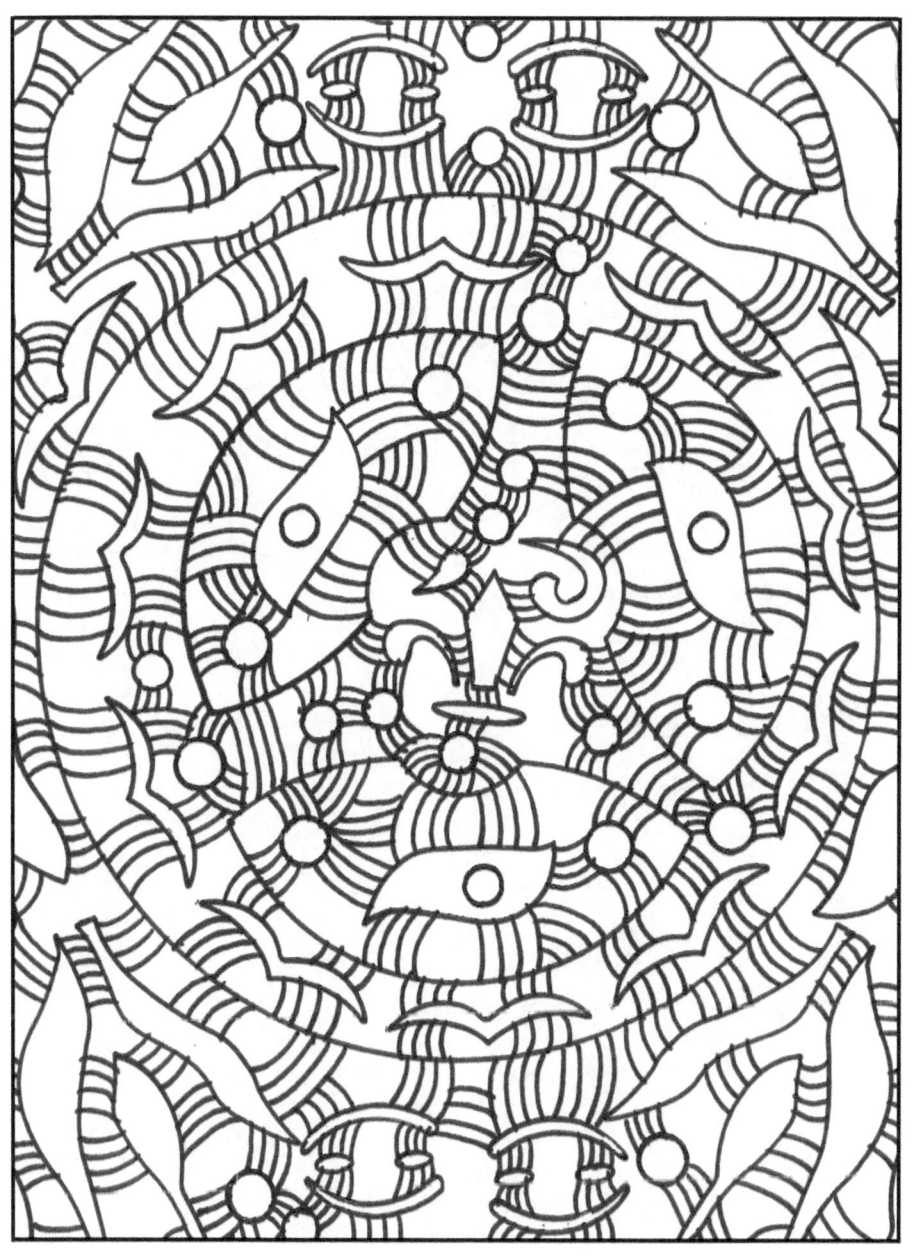

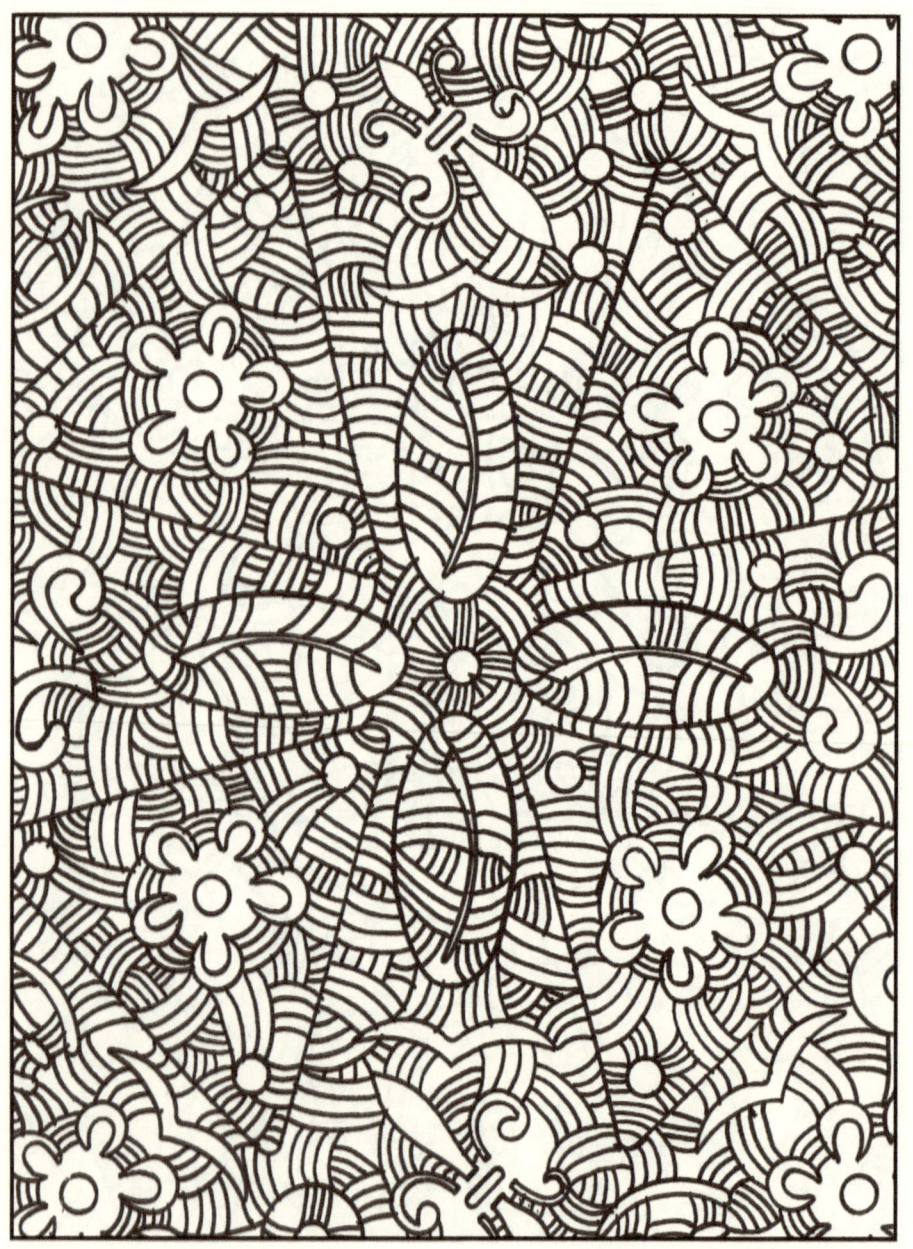

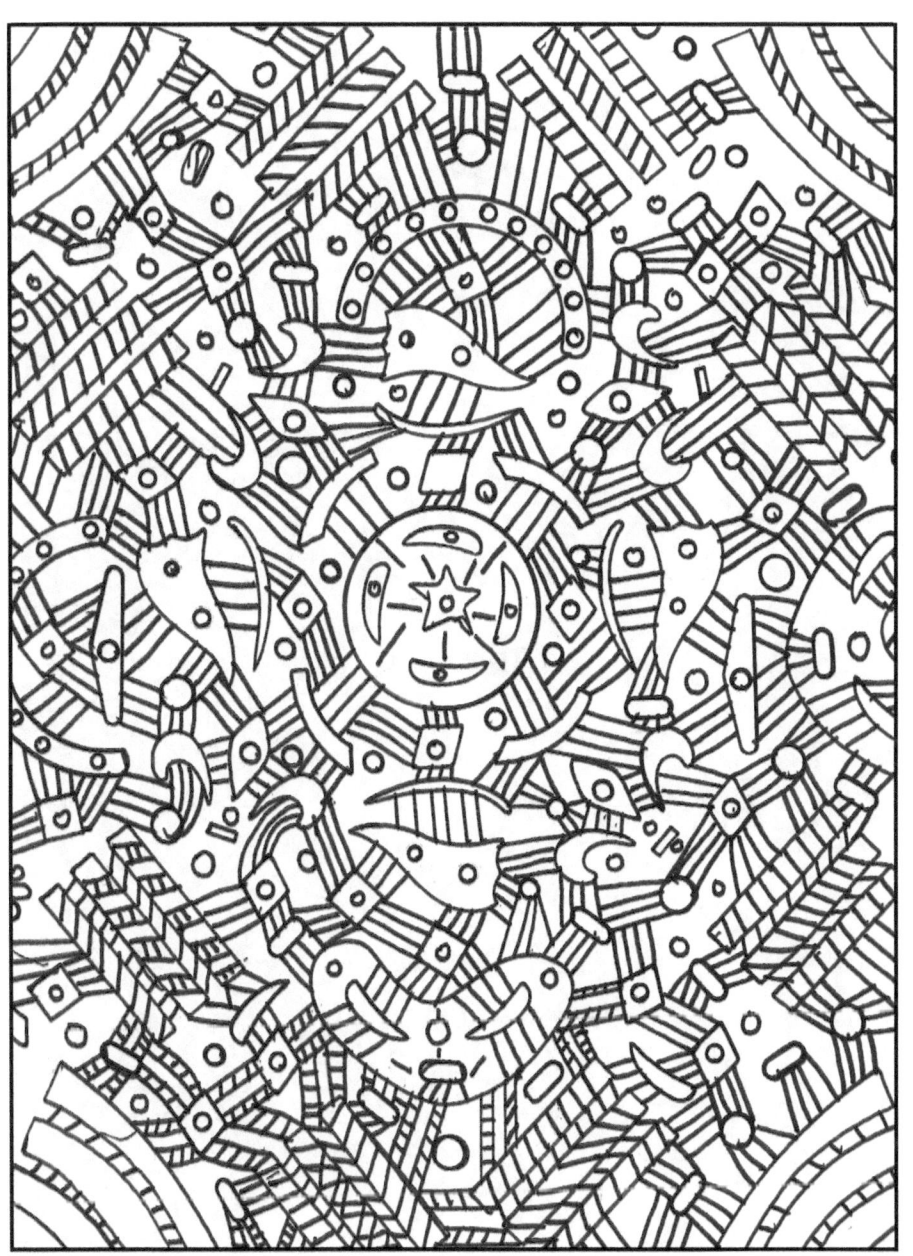

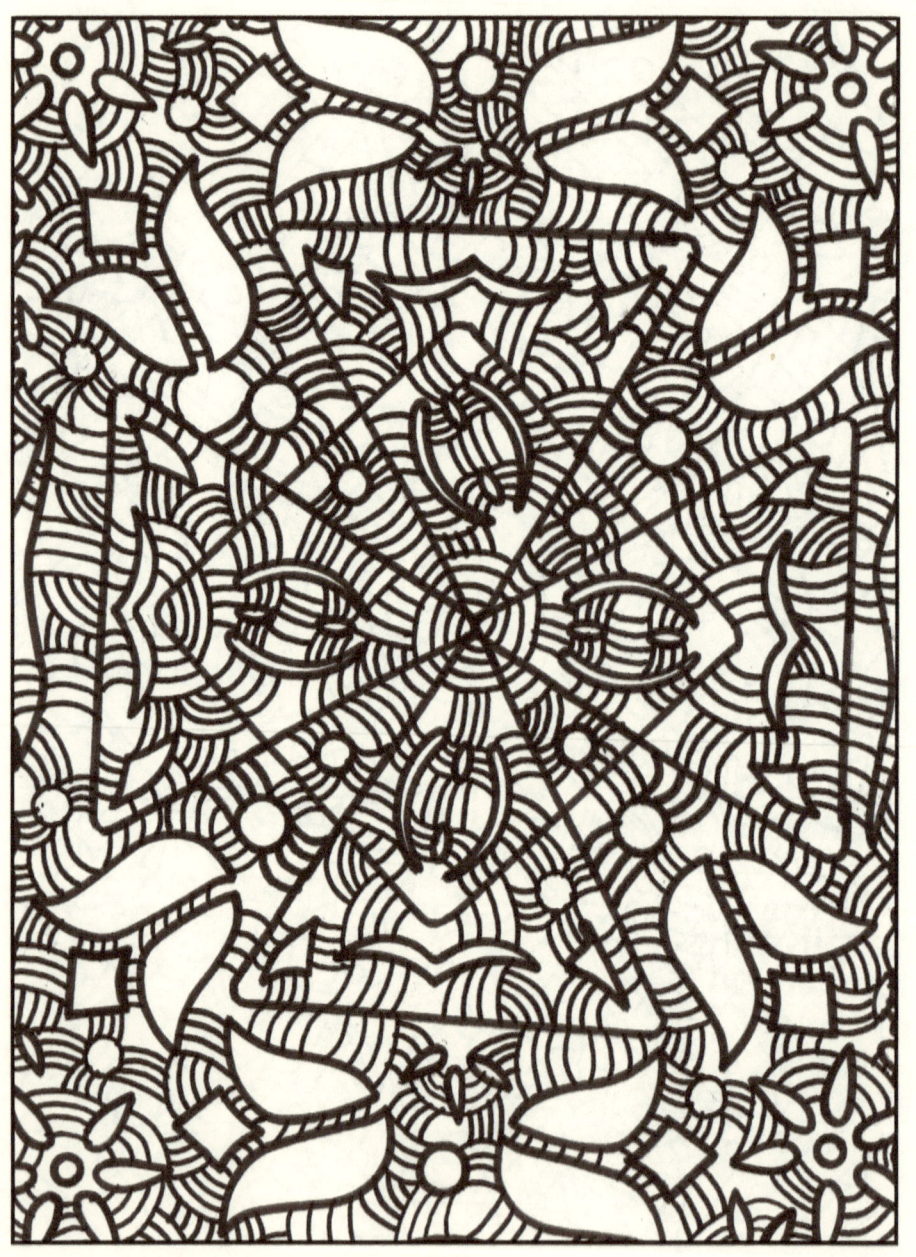

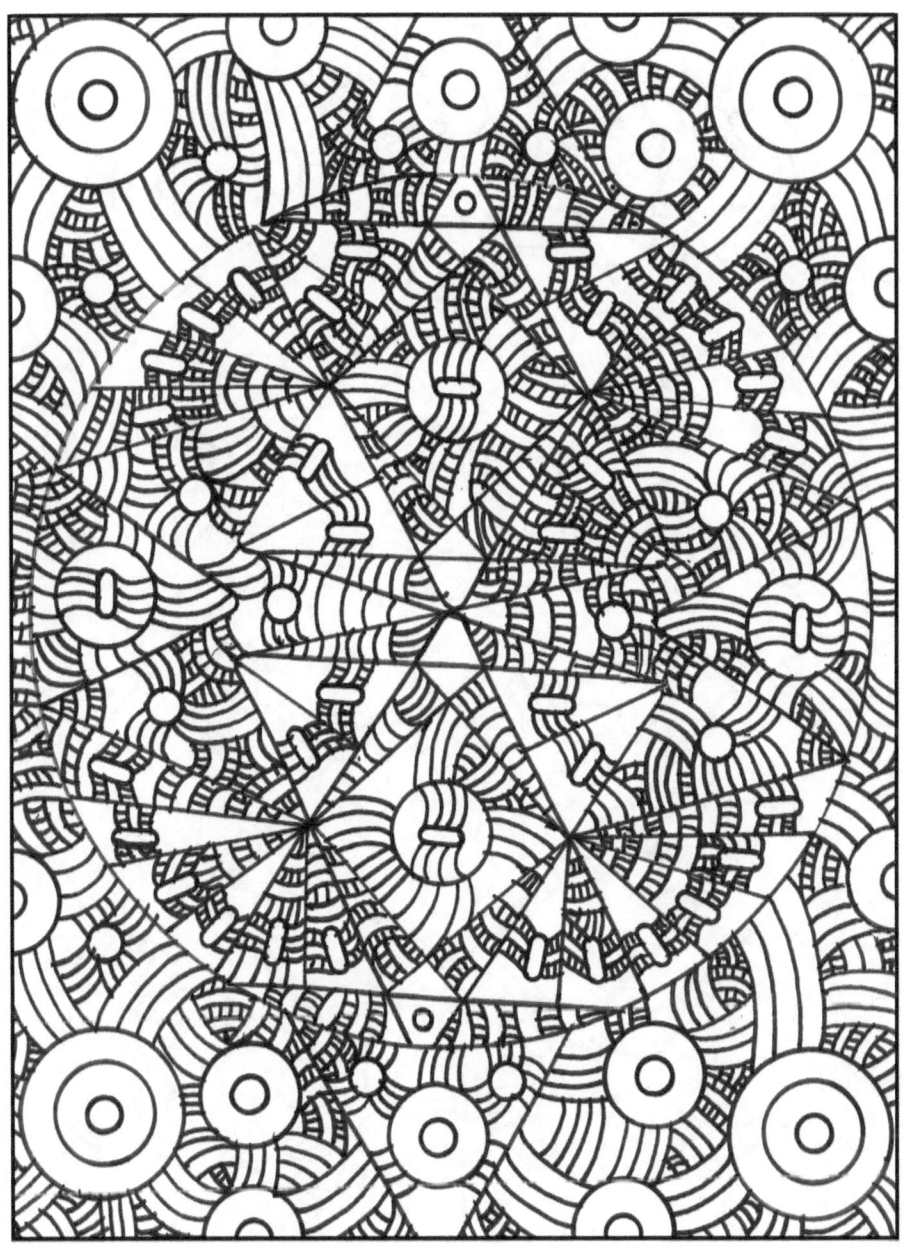

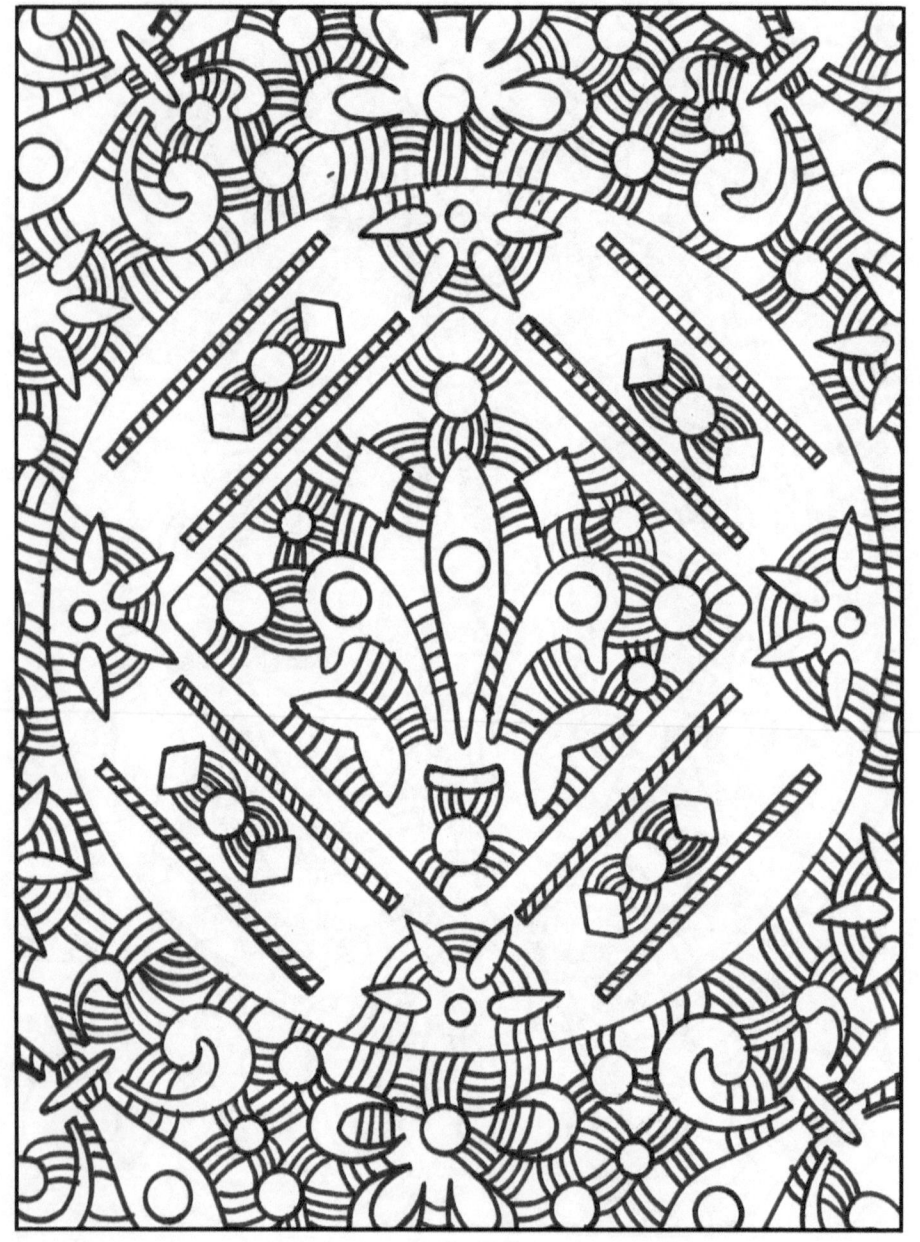

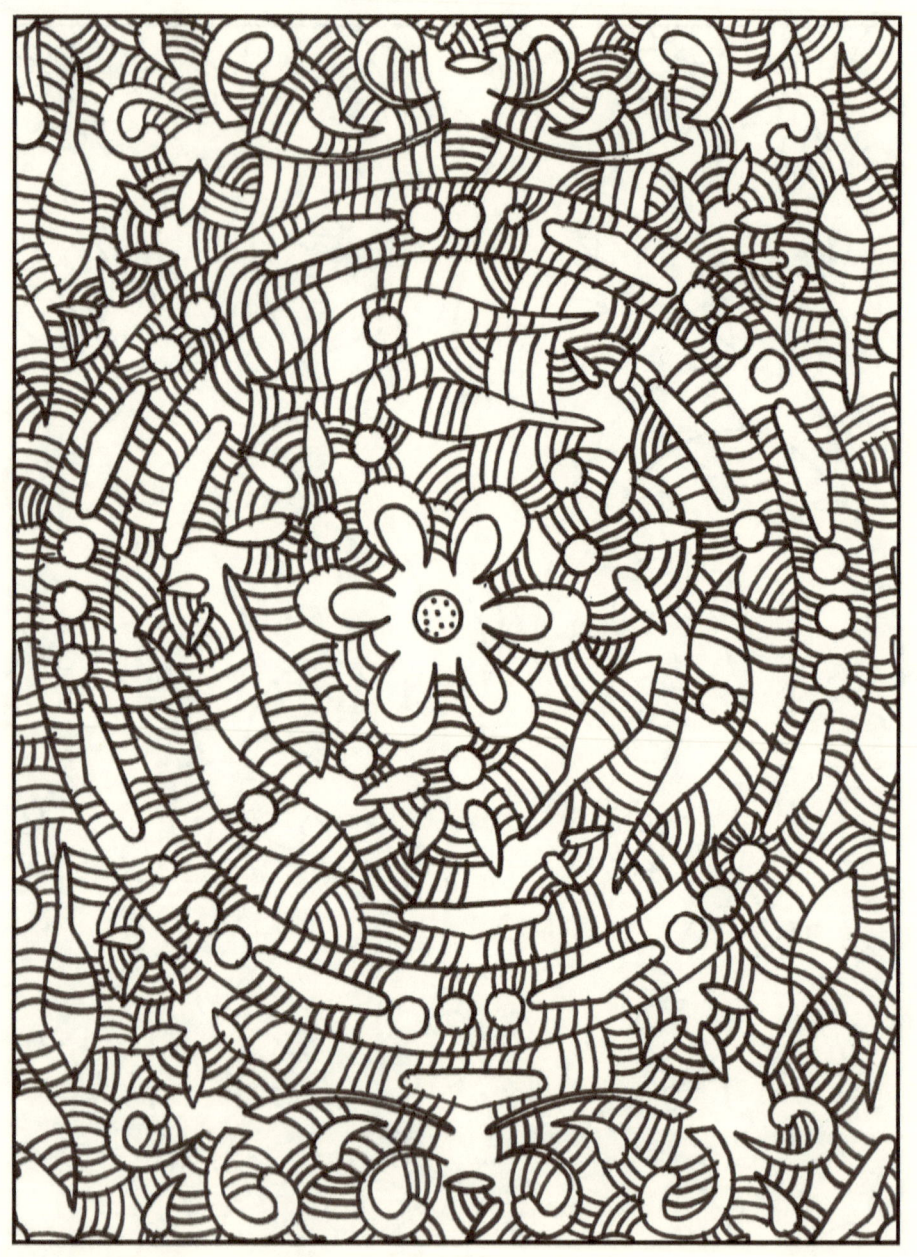

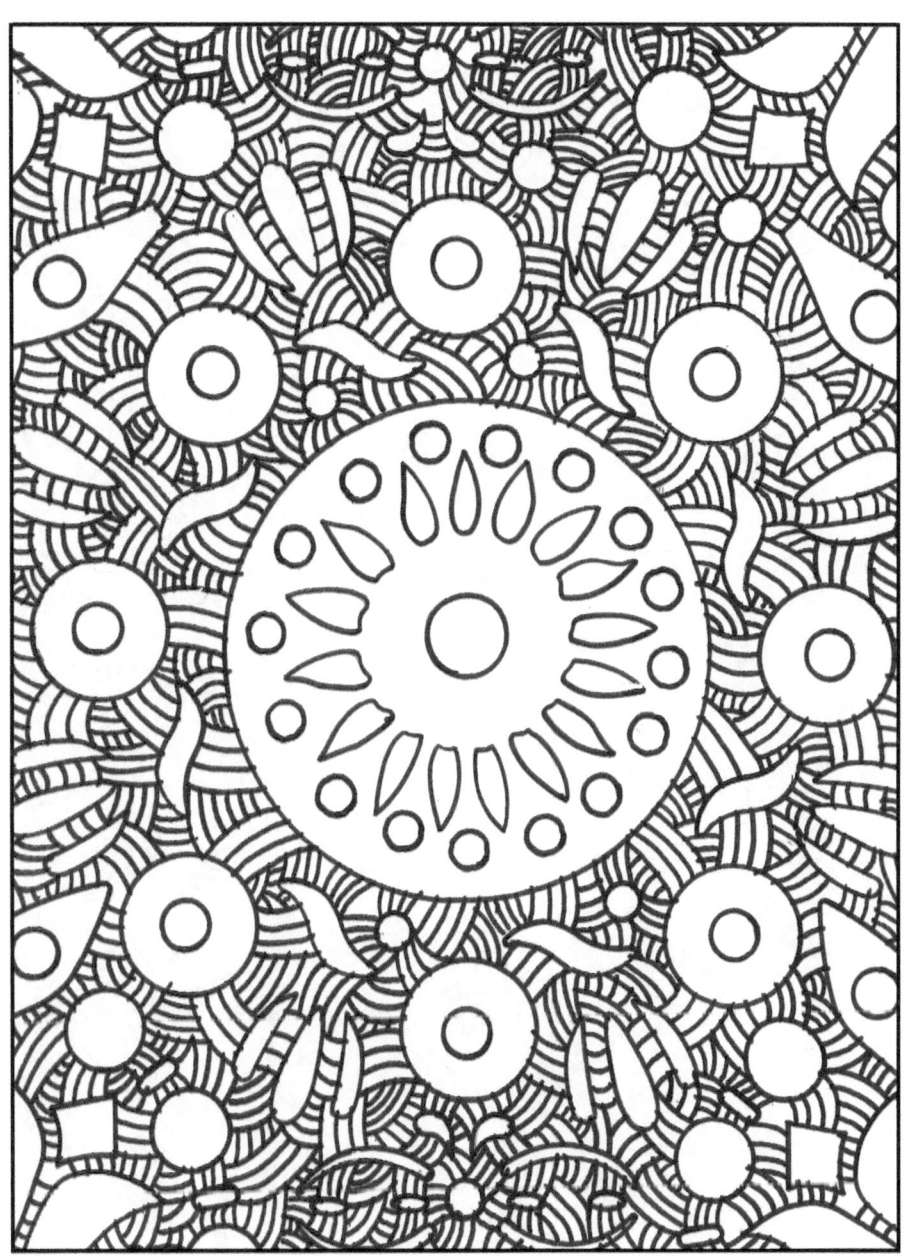

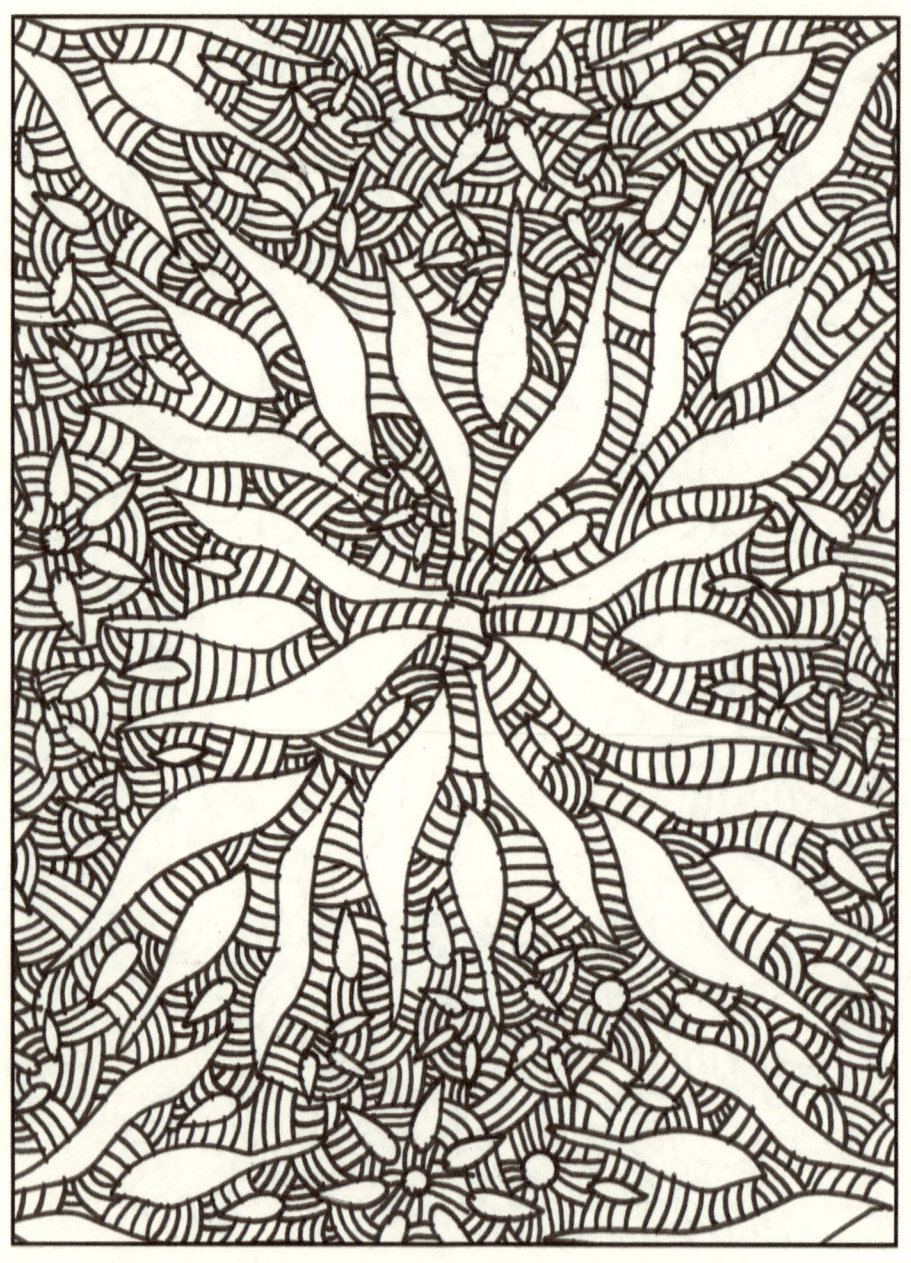

90

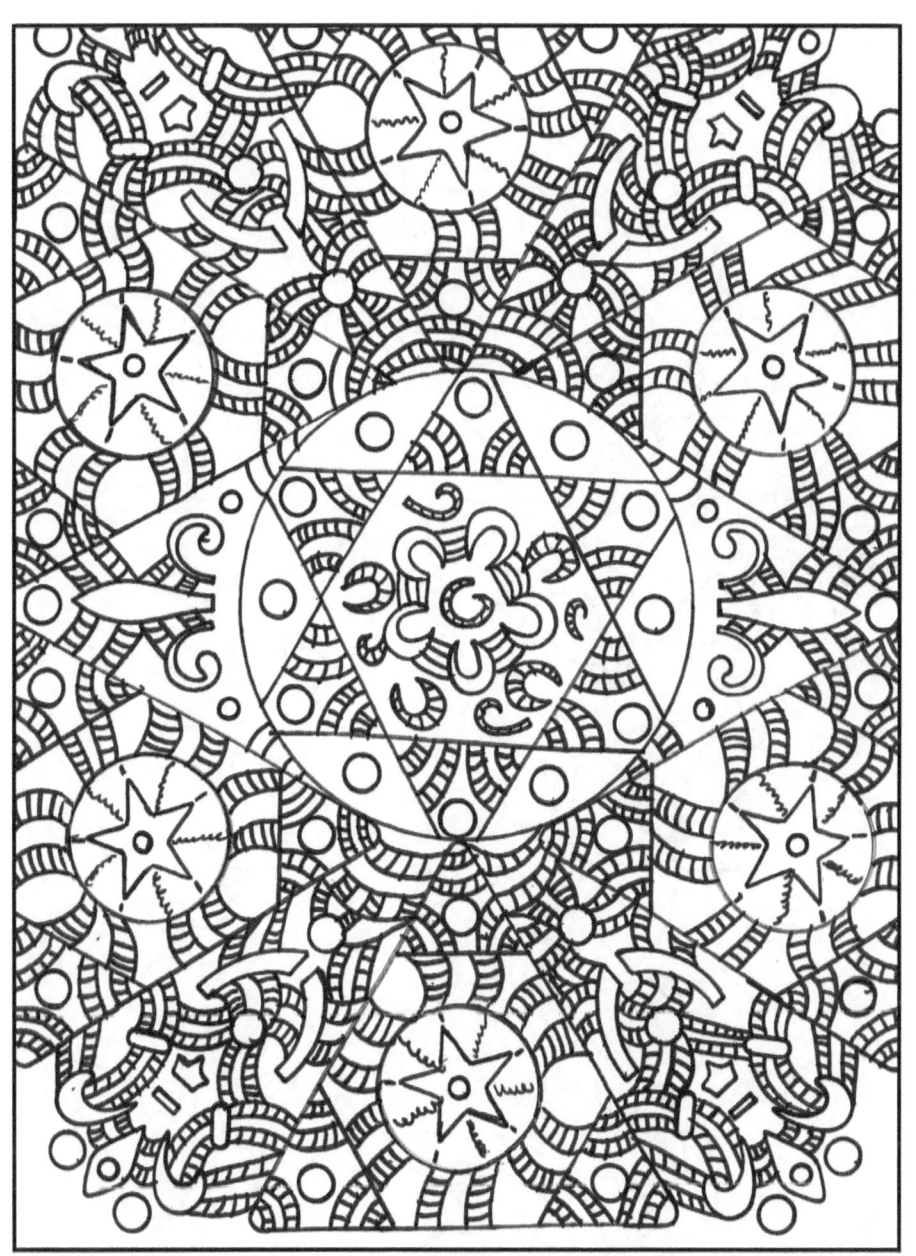

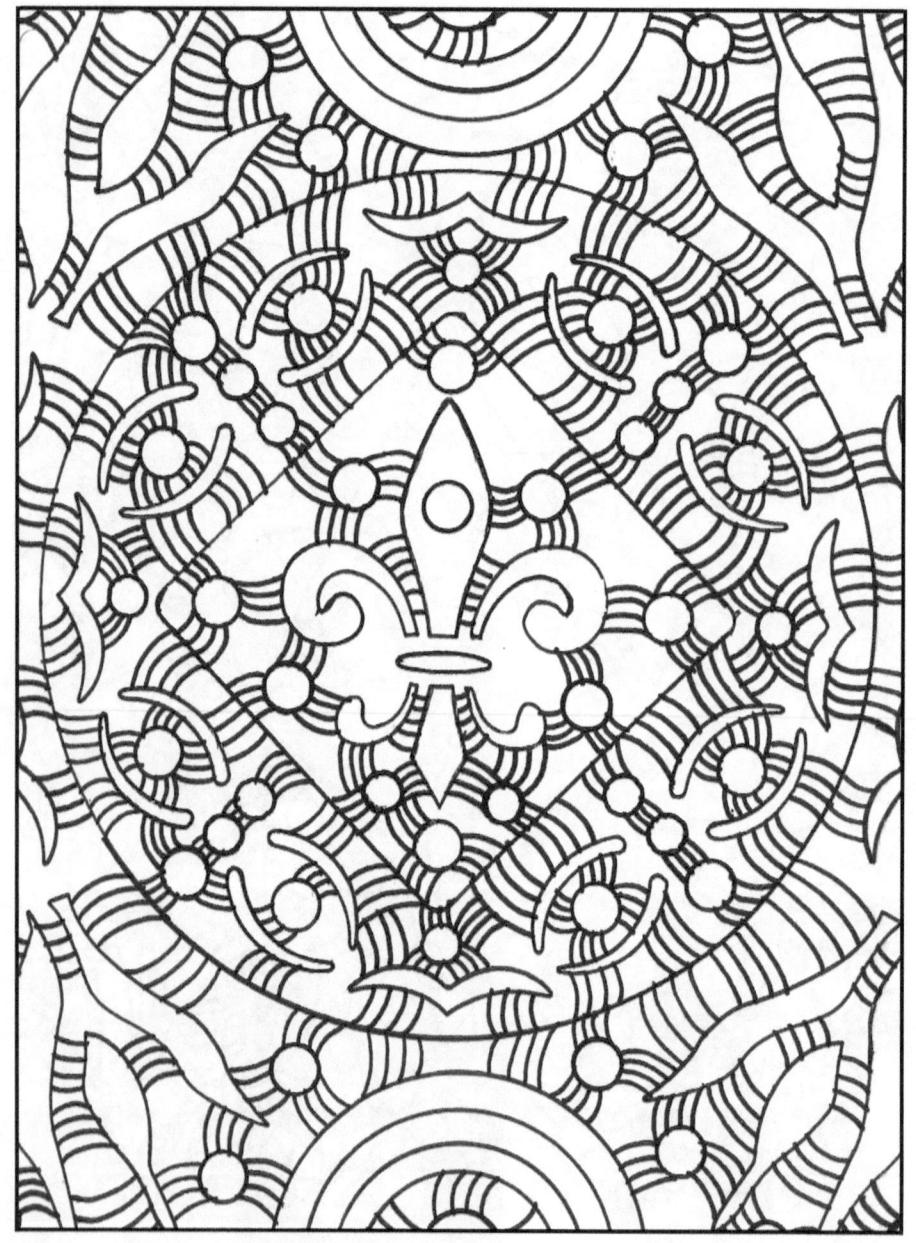

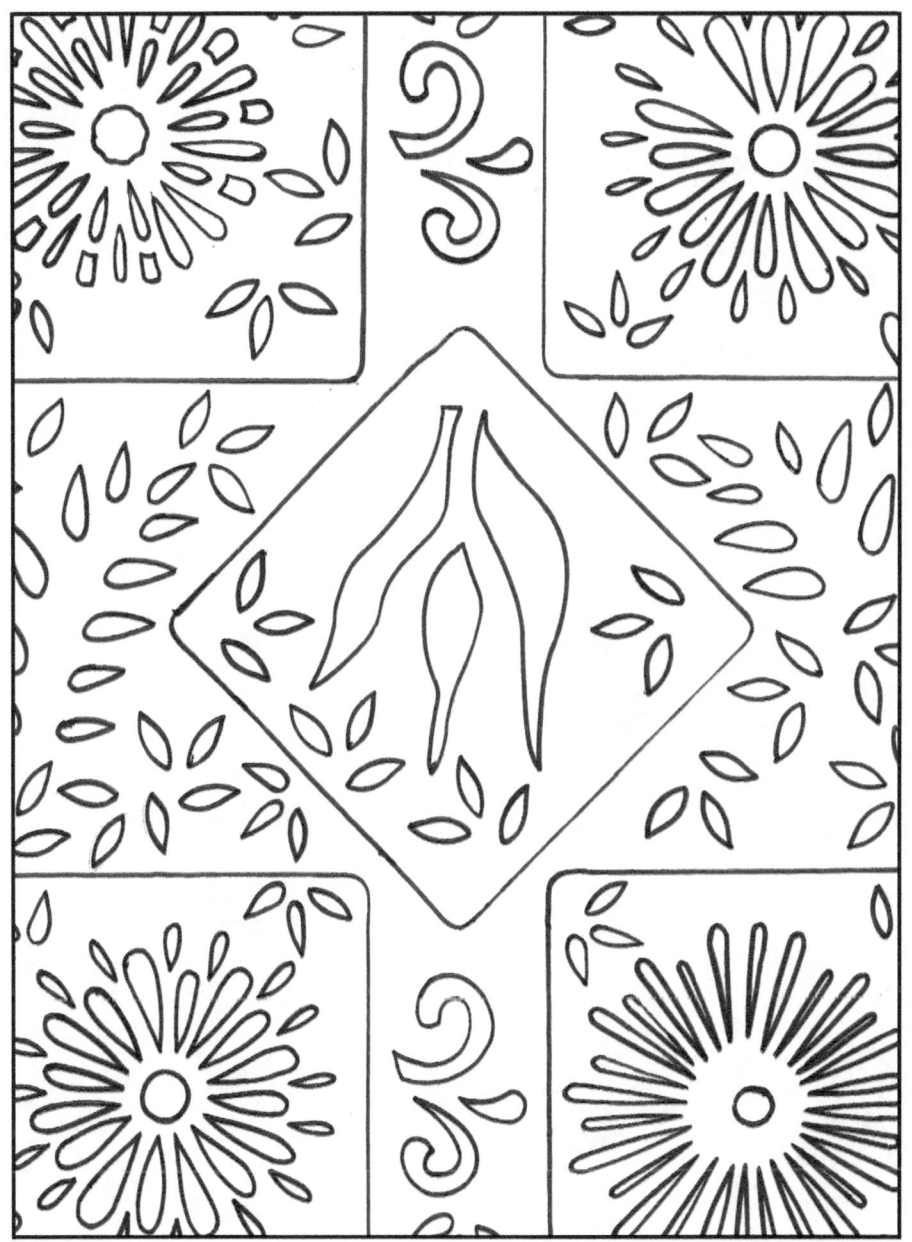

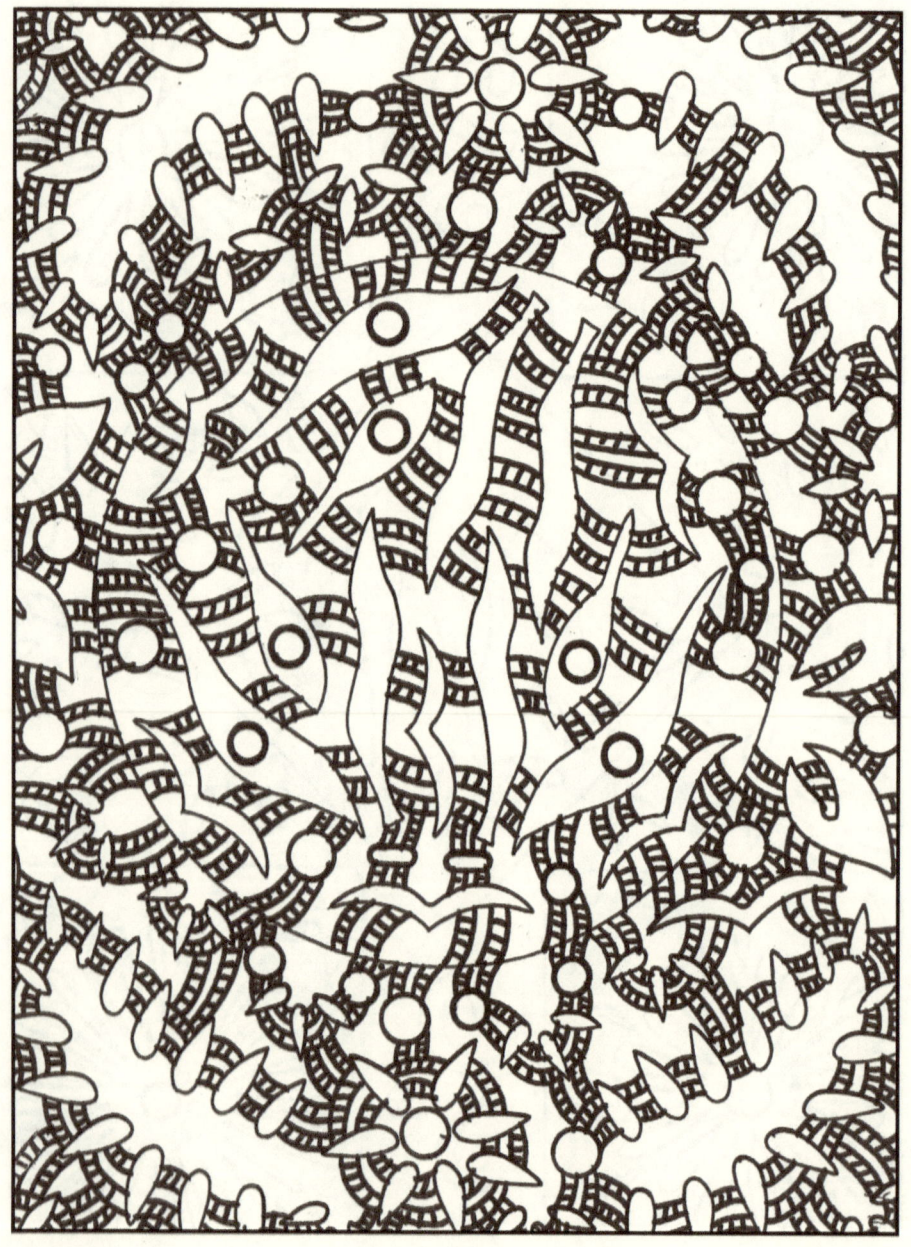

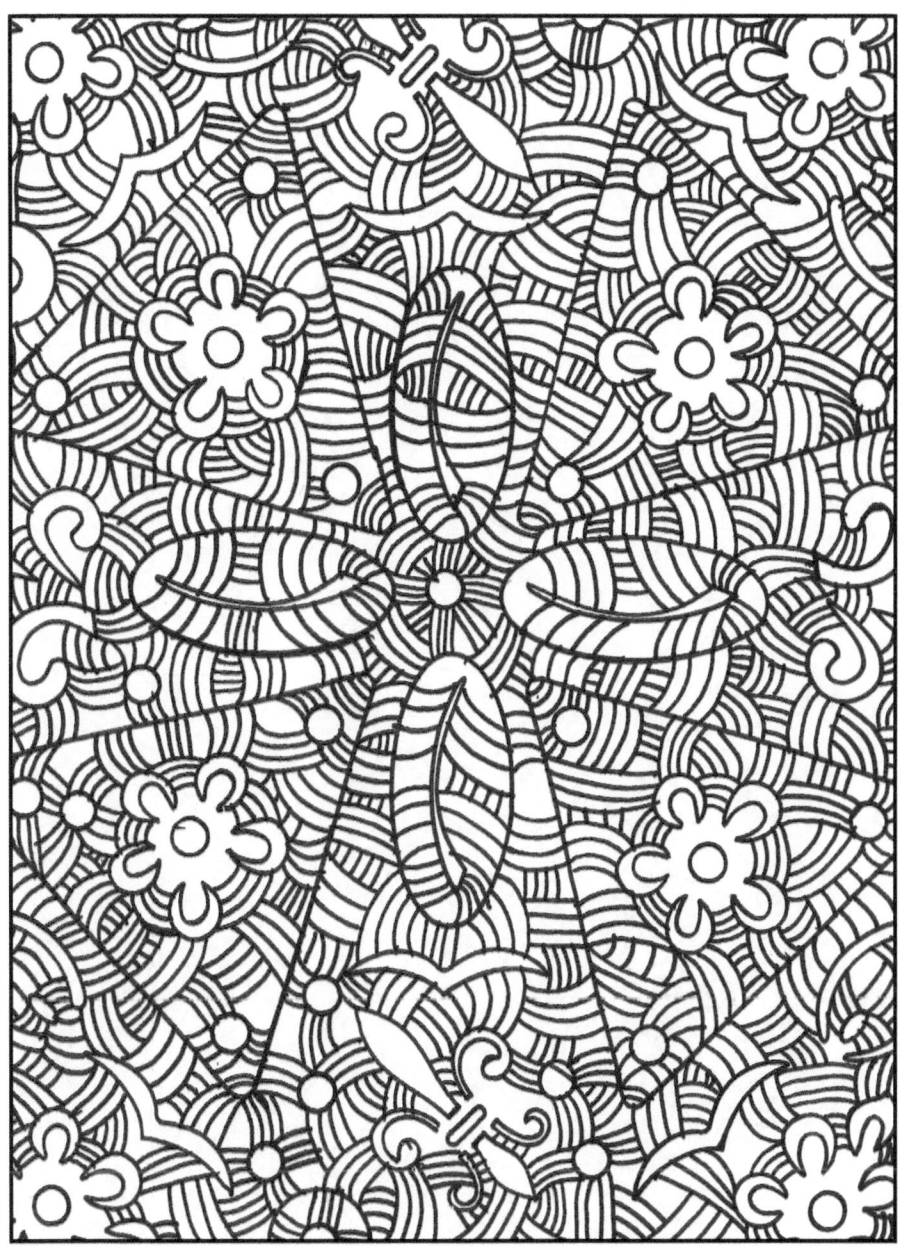

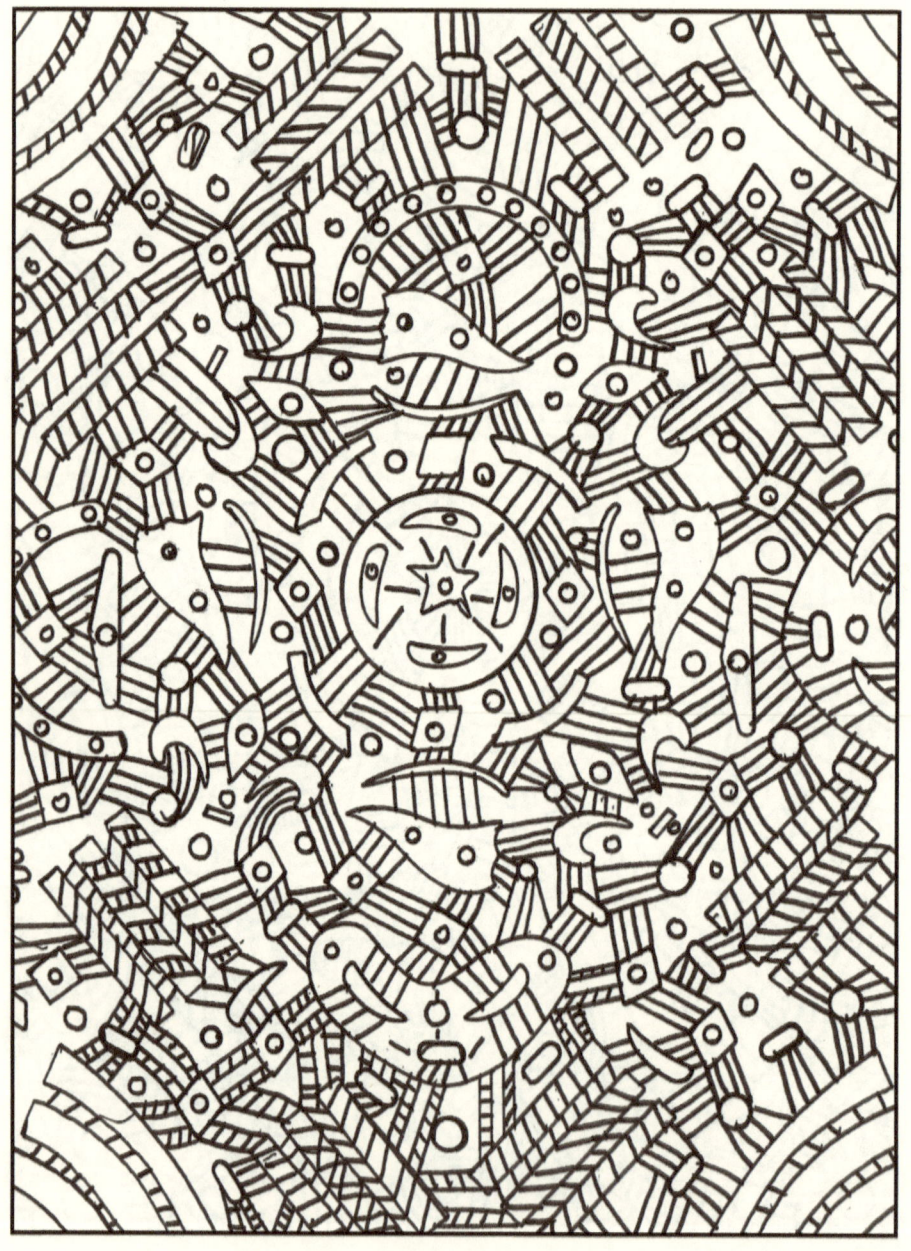

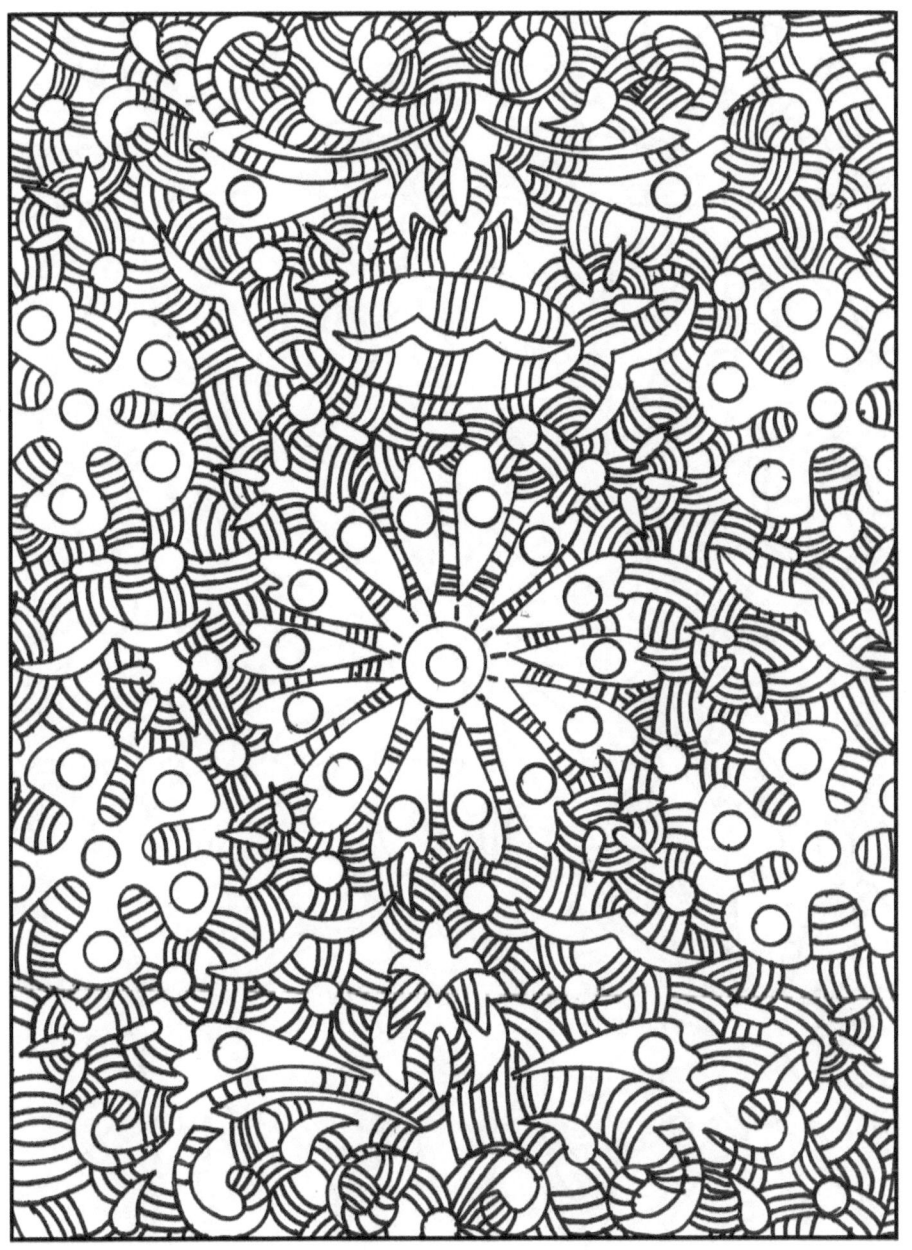

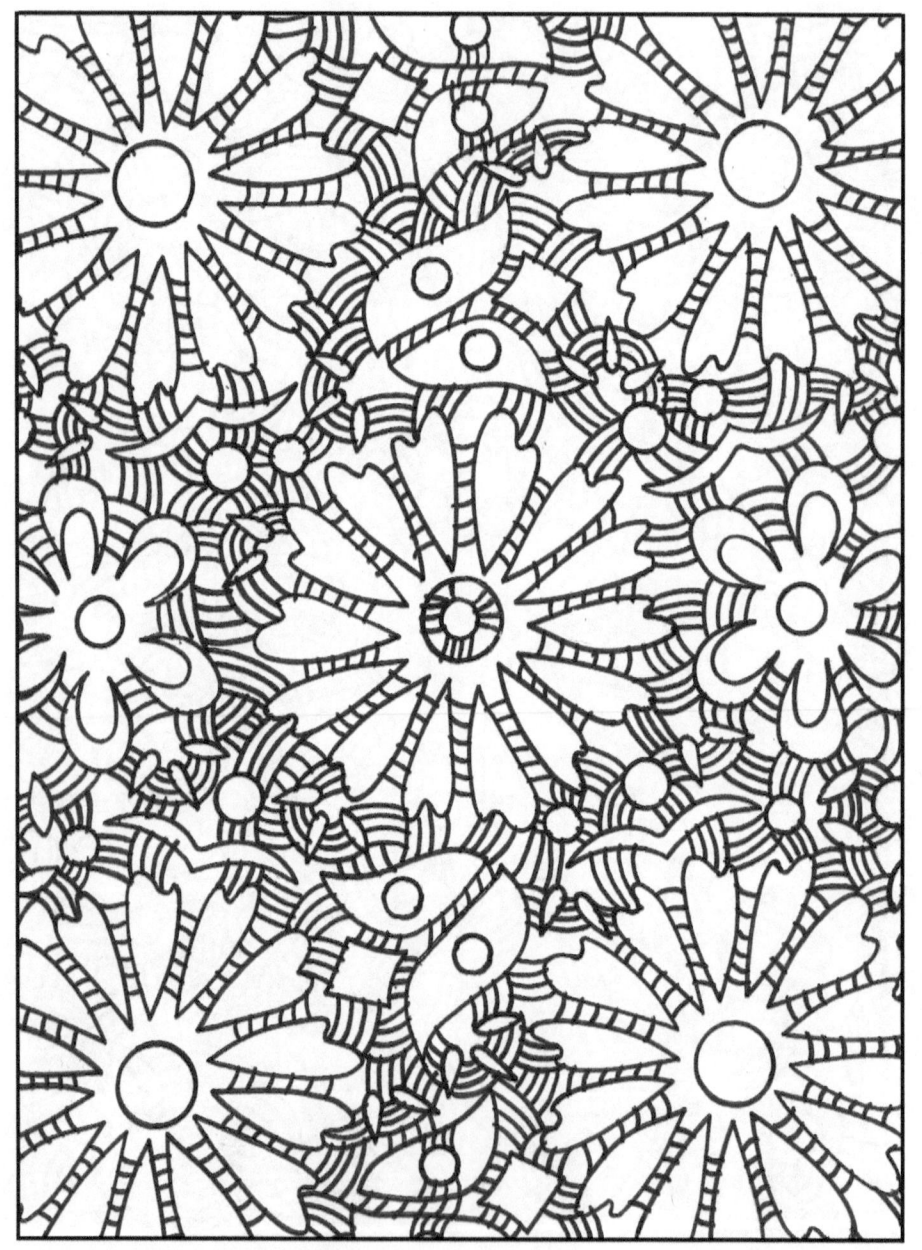

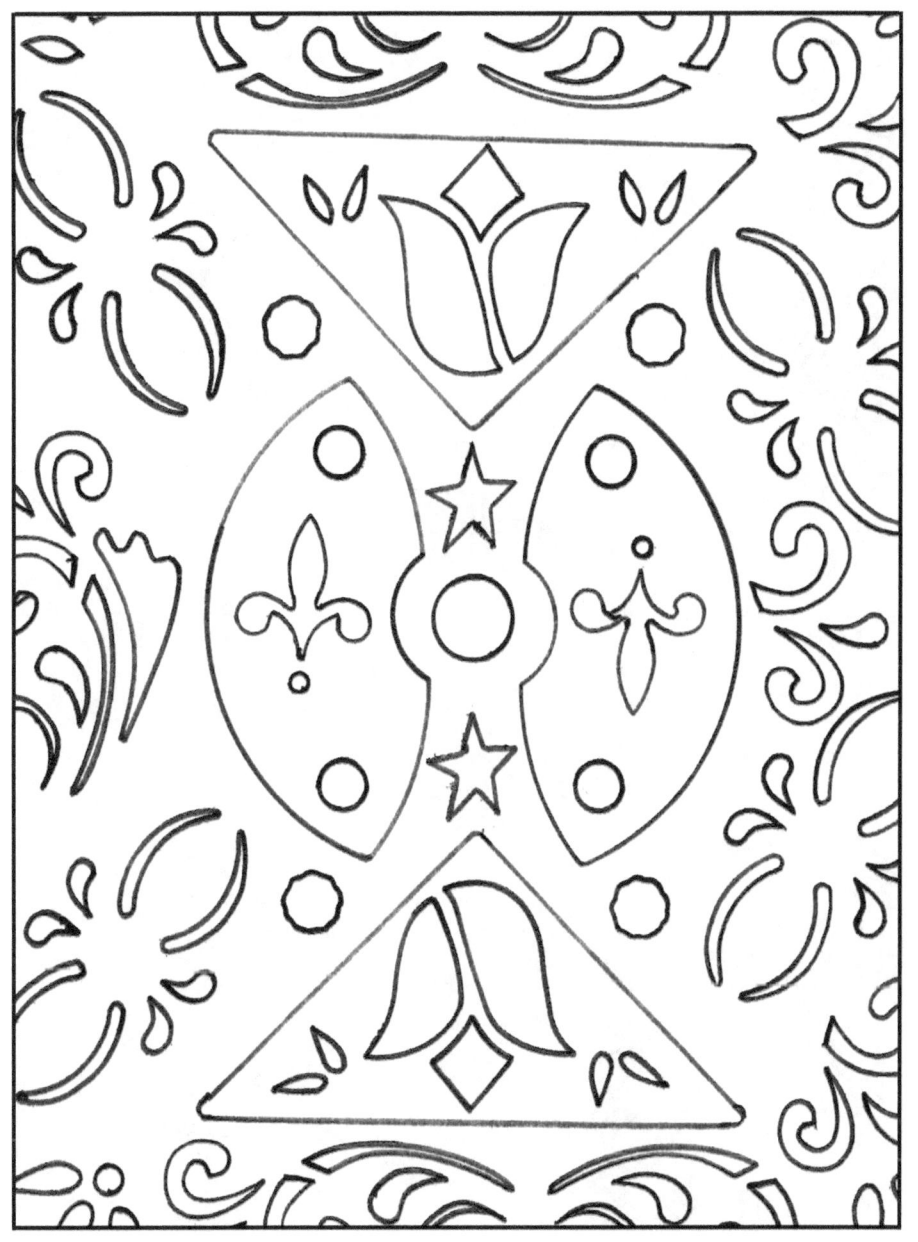

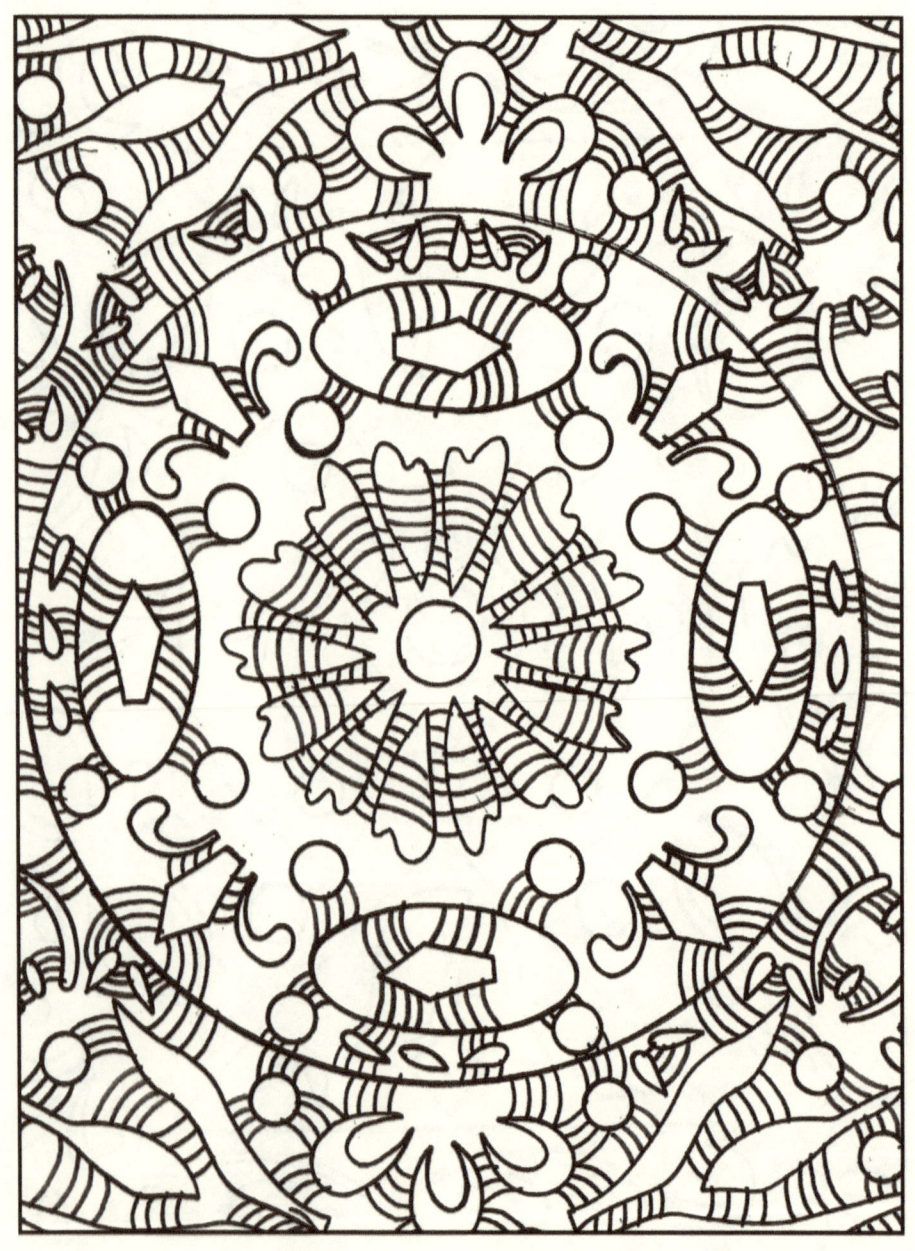

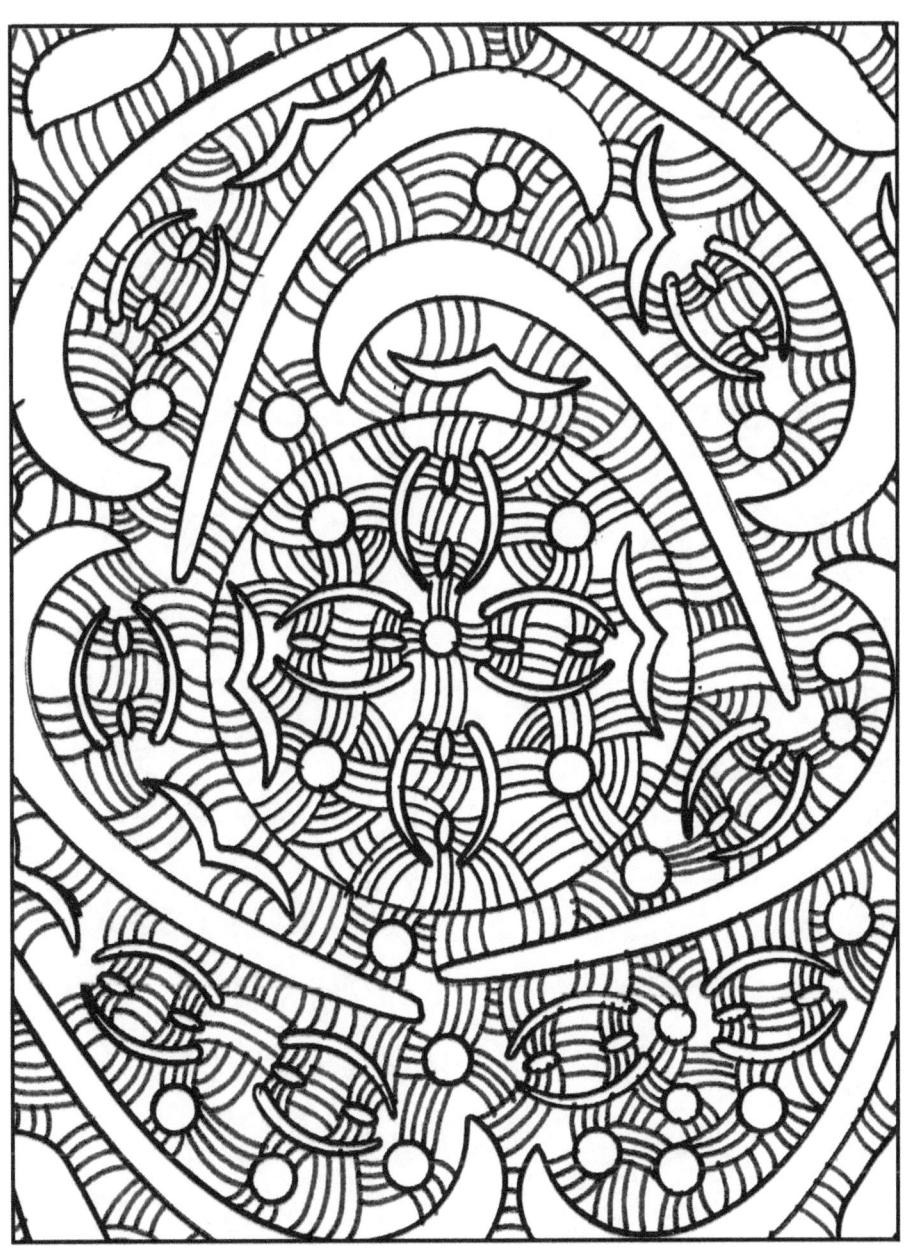

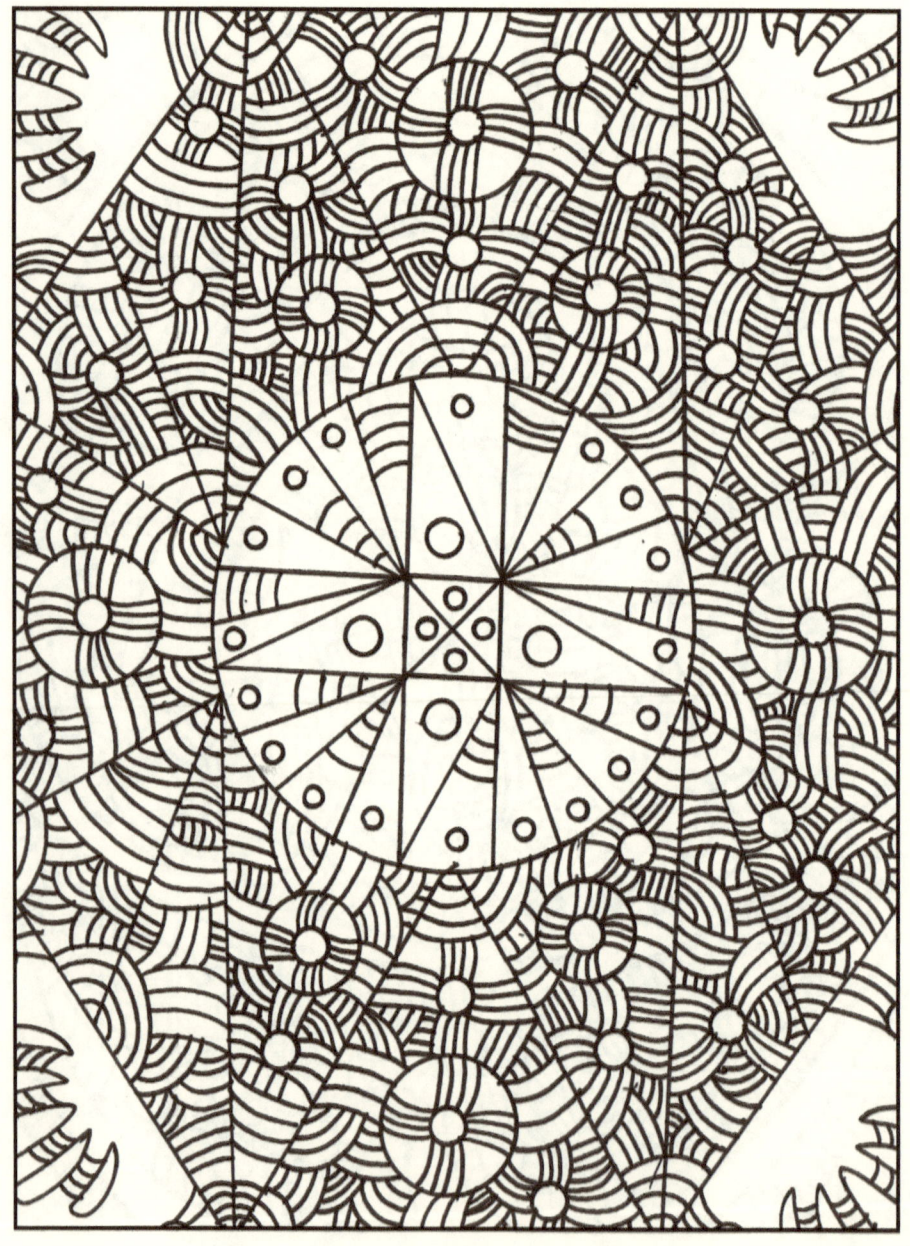

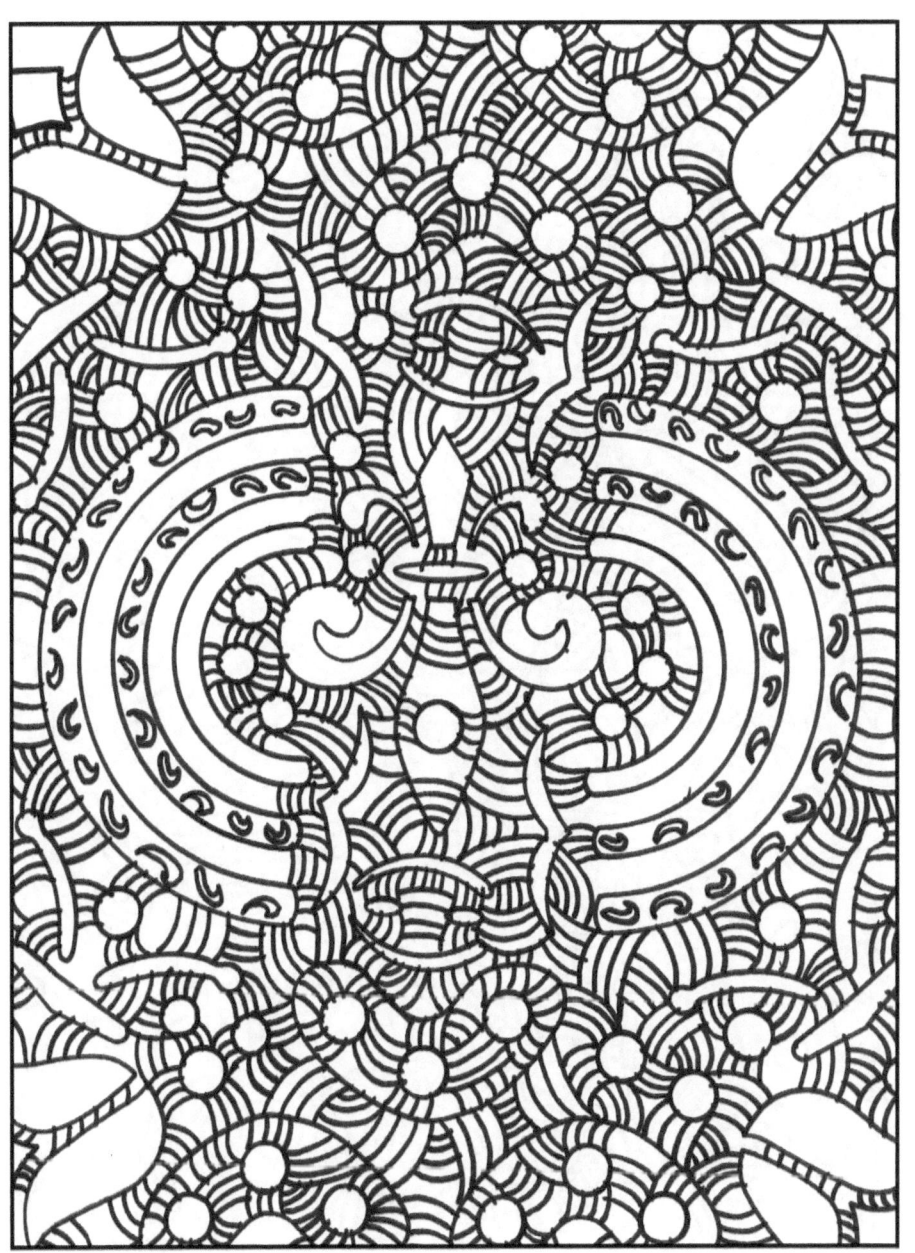

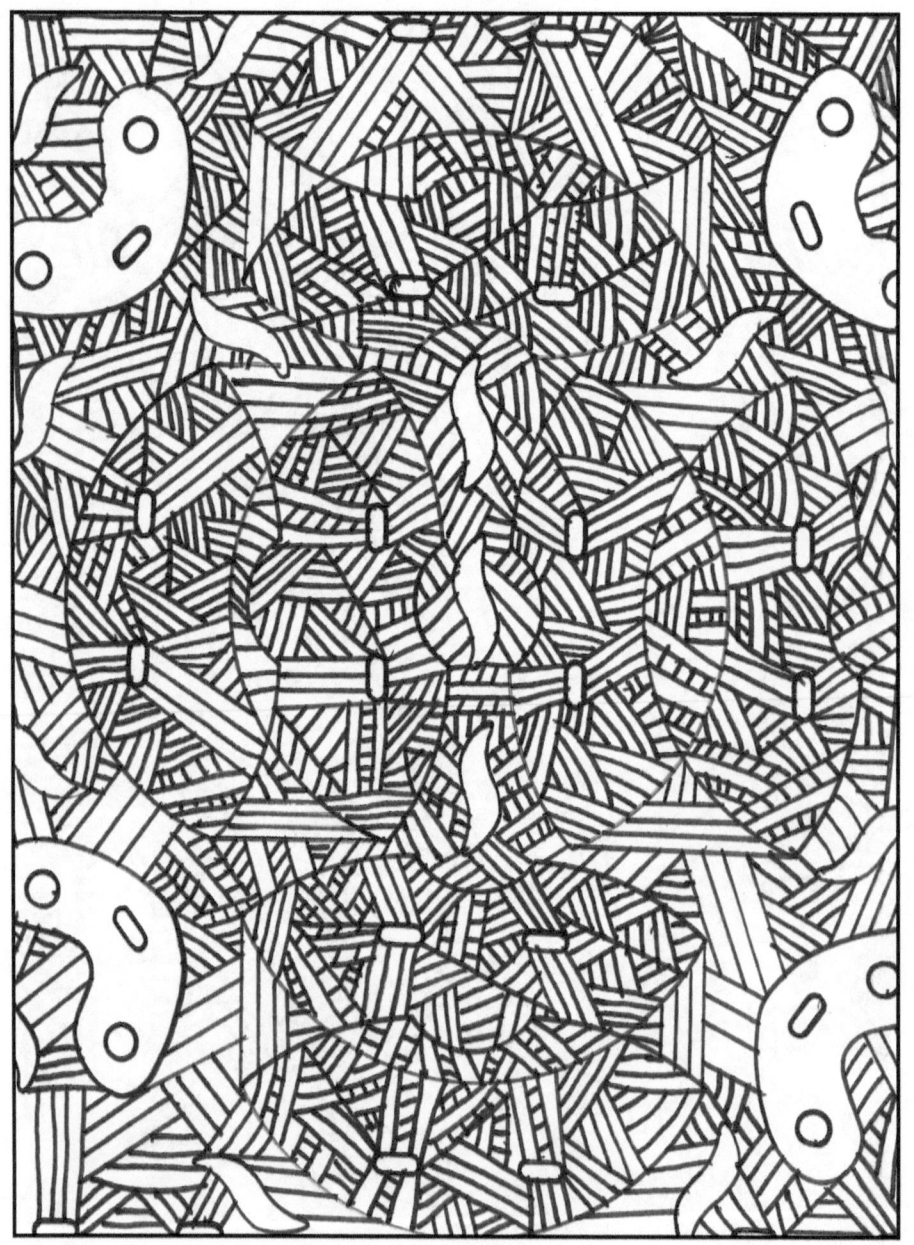

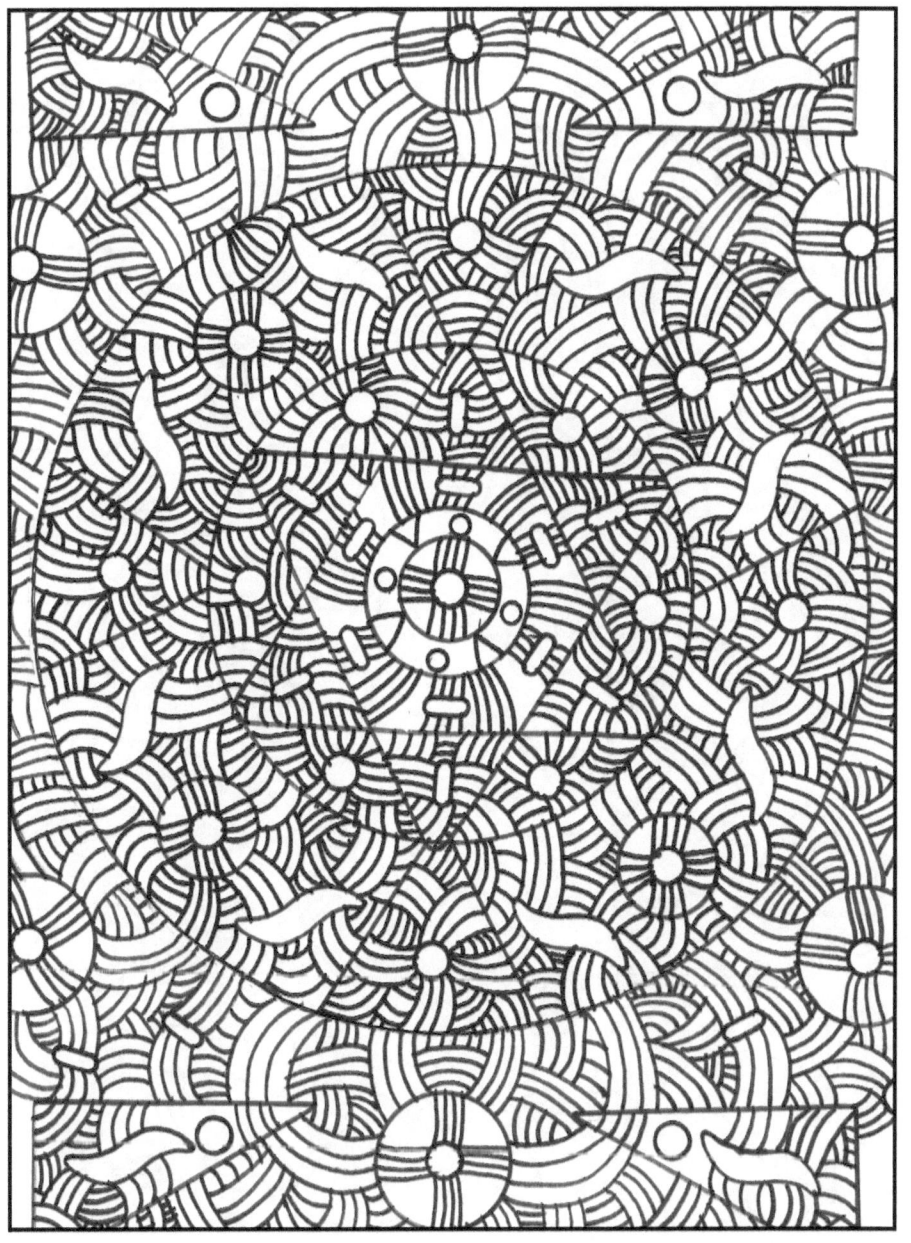

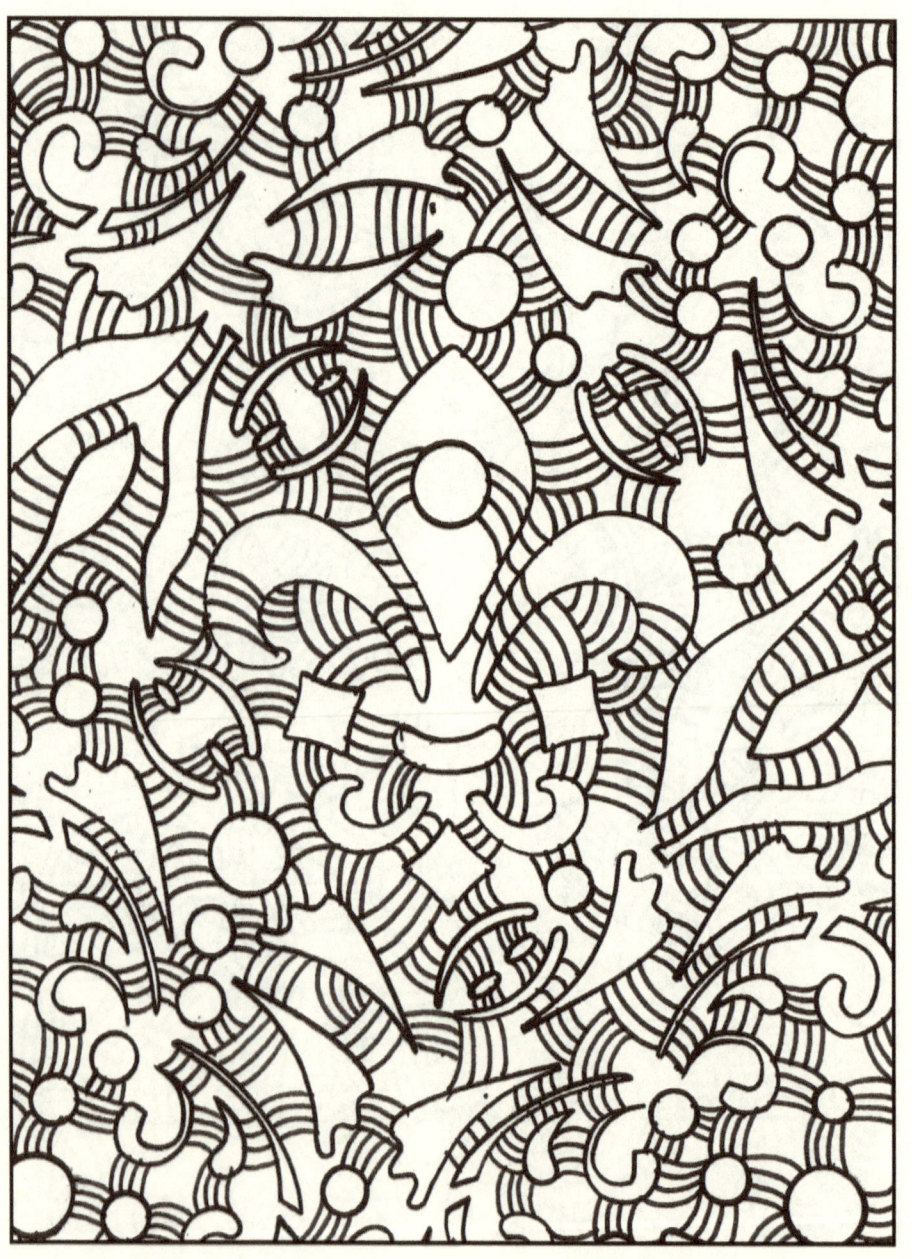

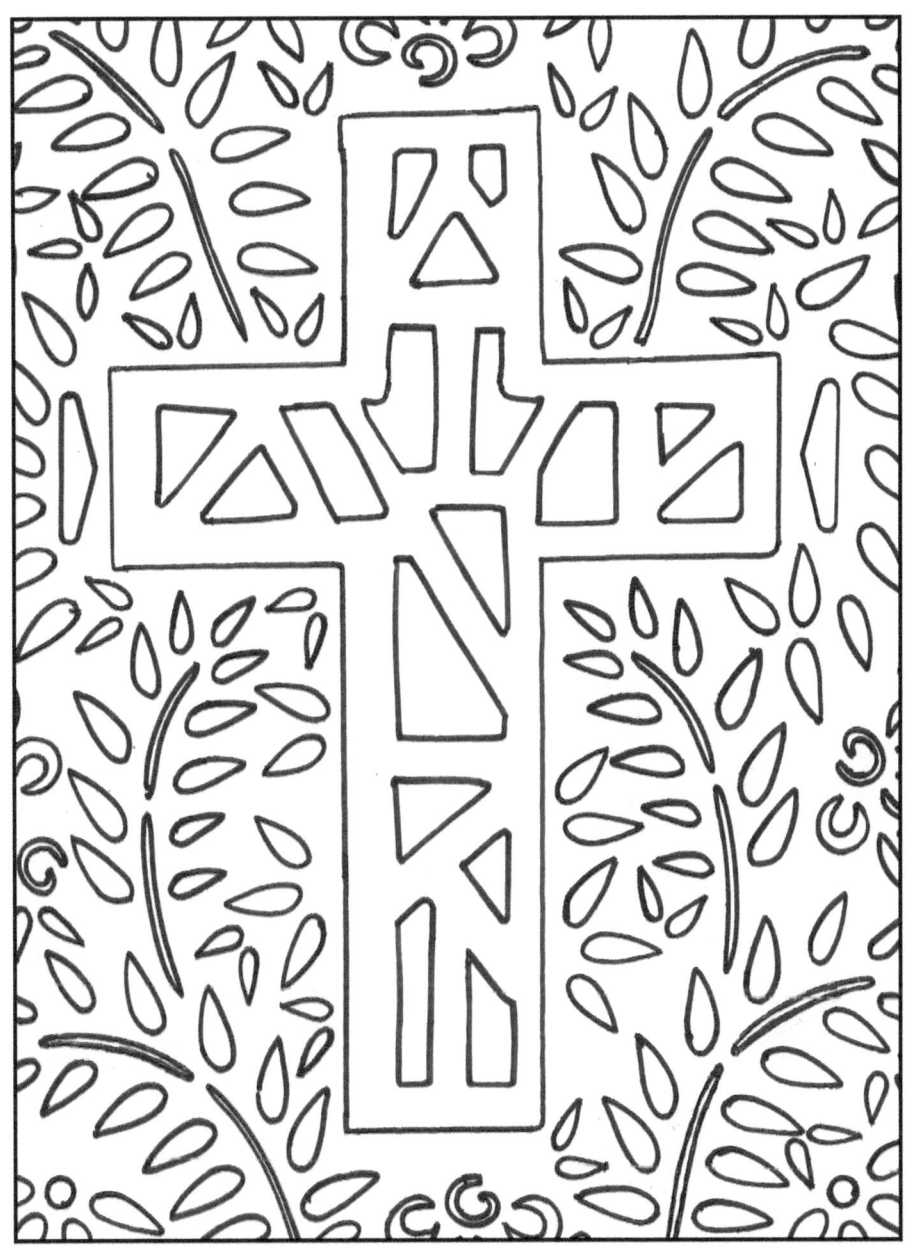

www.ingramcontent.com/pod-product-compliance
Lightning Source LLC
Chambersburg PA
CBHW022104170526
45157CB00004B/1471